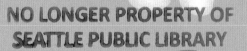

Pasta for All Seasons

Pasta <u>for</u> All Seasons

Dishes That Celebrate the
Flavors of Italy and the Bounty
of the Pacific Northwest

Michela Tartaglia

Photography by Kyle Johnson
Illustrations by Daniele Simonelli

≋ SASQUATCH BOOKS | SEATTLE

For Viola Rosa and Eva Luna, *i miei amori più grandi*

Contents

60   *Paccheri con tonno alalunga fresco, melanzane, capperi e menta /* **Paccheri with Wild Pacific Northwest Albacore Tuna, Eggplant, Capers, and Mint**

62   *Ziti con pesto di rucola, zenzero e noci, ricotta salata e olio di peperoncino habanero /* **Ziti with Arugula, Ginger, and Walnut Pesto, Ricotta Salata, and Red Habanero Chili Oil**

63   *Fusilli con zucchine, limone, menta, mandorle tostate e fiori di zucca fritti /* **Fusilli with Zucchini, Lemon, Mint, Toasted Almonds, and Fried Zucchini Blossoms**

67   *Creste di gallo con crema di peperone giallo, ricotta salata, friggitelli e pepe di Aleppo /* **Creste di Gallo with Yellow Bell Pepper Puree, Ricotta Salata, Shishito Peppers, and Aleppo Pepper**

70   *Casarecce con granchio del Pacific Northwest, asparagi e zenzero /* **Casarecce with Pacific Northwest Crab, Asparagus, and Ginger**

72   *Tagliolini con caviale di salmone al profumo di limone e pepe Szechuan /* **Tagliolini with Salmon Roe Caviar, Lemon, and Sichuan Pepper**

75   *Bucatini all'amatriciana con pomodori cimelio di Billy /* **Bucatini all'Amatriciana with Billy's Heirloom Tomatoes**

78   *Creste di gallo con melanzane, 'nduja, pomodorini e ricotta salata /* **Creste di Gallo with Eggplant, 'Nduja, Supersweet Tomatoes, and Ricotta Salata**

81   *Pipe con salsiccia all'uva di Chelan e rosmarino /* **Pipe with Local Sausage, Chelan Grapes, and Rosemary**

FALL
83

WINTER 109

Introduction

Pasta every day. Pasta in all its glorious forms, textures, and shapes. Pasta for your body, pasta for your brain, but, really, it's about pasta for your *soul*. Per capita, Italians eat an average of sixty-two pounds of pasta annually, which means tucking into a plate of pasta goodness three to four times a week. We eat it mainly for lunch, but it's certainly on the menu for dinner as well. It's a national point of pride, "an icon of Italian cooking" (says Massimo Montanari in *A Short History of Spaghetti with Tomato Sauce*), and something that we could never give up. And why would we want to?

Not to sound dramatic, but I literally cannot imagine my life without a bowl of pasta in it. It's never boring because when you add fresh, seasonal ingredients, the possibilities (pasta-bilities?) are limitless.

Don't get me wrong. You can have an excellent pasta, but with a lackluster or pedestrian sauce, your dish is ruined. Or you can cook a wonderful sauce, but combined with a poor-quality pasta, the result will be subpar.

This small but mighty publication is unmistakably a pasta book, but the fresh ingredients—particularly ingredients from the Pacific Northwest (or PNW, as we affectionately call it)—are the stars of the show.

When we opened Pasta Casalinga in Pike Place Market, we wanted to focus on fresh pasta making, crafted in small batches, created with quality flour and perfectly cooked al dente. And we wanted to lean into local and seasonal ingredients, from the stinging nettles that appear all over the Olympic Peninsula and around

the Seattle area during springtime to the Pacific golden chanterelles in the fall.

Here, you will find my favorite local ingredients paired with pasta. The chapters are organized by season and the recipes are labeled with icons to indicate whether they are ≋ *from the ocean* (featuring seafood), 🏛 *from the farm* (featuring raised meats), or 🌱 *from the garden* (all vegetarian). In other words, there is a pasta option for everyone.

Cooking seasonally and, therefore, eating seasonally has always been the only choice in my family. I grew up in a small town near Turin in the Piedmont region of Italy before globalization, which meant having asparagus exclusively in the spring and green beans only in the summertime. I am grateful for my upbringing because I learned the importance of knowing where your food comes from and when it is available. For me, that translates into refusing to eat

certain foods at certain times of the year. Asparagus in December? Inconceivable!

The dishes here are not secret family recipes, which are often what's valued when talking about Italian cooking. Is it my *nonna's* recipe? Is it going to taste like it came from the streets of Naples? Sometimes yes but mostly no. Infused with my Italian sensibilities, culture, and training, these recipes are a tribute to the PNW and combine classic flavors with creative twists designed to showcase the local bounty. Italian through and through, I am a pasta lover who is continually inspired to cook with the seasons. I hope that they can encourage you to let the ingredients be your guide when cooking and to find many ways to incorporate fresh produce, seafood, and meats into pasta dishes. It's the best way to feed your soul.

A Pasta Primer

Fresh, dried, long, short, flat, wide, smooth, ruffled, filled, with eggs, and without eggs.

Pasta comes in hundreds of shapes and textures. As you can imagine, it has a wonderful and rich history, and a passionate culture around it. There's even a museum devoted to pasta in Rome. Beautiful books have been published on the subject: several of them can show you how to make pasta and others can tell you everything about its origins. I'm going to focus here not on pasta making but instead on the Pacific Northwest ingredients. These recipes are approachable and straightforward, nothing fussy or complicated here. They all follow the same format: first make your sauce, then cook your pasta, and finally mix them together.

Pasta should be simple and never intimidating.

I tried to be as accurate as I could, despite being a native Italian writer, and I attempted to err on the side of less is more for *quanto basta*, which author Missy Robbins translates to "as much as you like, as much as you need." Italian recipes are traditionally a little less detailed, allowing the cook to bring their own preferences to the table. Always feel free to adjust the herbs, spices, Parmigiano, and olive oil to your taste (note that for finishing, these aren't accounted for in the ingredients). Lastly, although you may already know the modus operandi when it comes to cooking pasta, a few important reminders follow.

DOS AND DON'TS WHEN COOKING PASTA

DON'T! **Add oil to the water**

No olive oil whatsoever in the pasta water! The only time you should add a drizzle is if your son invites his soccer team over for dinner, and you want to cook pasta for them but you don't have a large enough pot. The oil will prevent the pasta from sticking together. It's an emergency technique that should be avoided in general because the pasta will get oily and will not adhere to its sauce when mixed.

DO! **Salt the water**

Pasta should always be cooked in *plenty* of boiling salted water. You can liberally salt the water whenever you want: at the beginning if you don't want to forget or right when it's boiling before cooking the pasta. Keep in mind that if you add the salt at the beginning, it will take slightly longer to boil because the water will be a little heavier.

You will need about 10 grams of salt per 1 liter (about 1 quart) of water, but always consider the saltiness of your sauce in order to maintain a balance between the two.

DO! **Keep the pasta water**

You should always reserve some cooking water when you drain your pasta for mixing into the sauce. That precious water is full of gluten, and it is a pure magic trick to help your pasta bind together. To avoid redundancy, I have not mentioned this in each recipe, but it's something you should do for all dishes in this book.

DON'T! Top sad drained pasta with sauce

Promise me that you will never, ever plop sauce on top of drained, pale-white plated pasta. All pasta should be tossed with its sauce before being served. The only job you should have when there's a pasta dish in front of you is to enjoy it, not assemble the components with each forkful. Since each pasta shape has a different cooking time, follow the package instructions for store-bought and check handmade pasta by tasting it.

DO! Use extra-virgin olive oil

There is very little space for butter in this book, with the exception of a knob of it in a ragù or sugo. Extra-virgin olive oil (EVOO) is everywhere in my recipes because it's the base of most, if not all, pasta sauces—not surprising for the king of the Mediterranean diet.

I am passionate about olive oil, as I was raised by an Italian family that has been producing EVOO for three generations. What's the difference between extra-virgin olive oil and olive oil? The first is barely processed pure juice that comes from olives, and nowadays, pretty much all the extra-virgin olive oil is cold-pressed, which helps it keep its nutritional value intact. EVOO is simply the best and should be used when cooking and making salad dressings. Olive oil, on the other hand, is a blend and is great for frying, due to its high amount of monounsaturated fat.

Always check where the olives are from—this disclosure must appear on the bottles. Often a "Spanish olive oil" is packed in Spain but is made with olives that come from different European countries (which is never a good indication of a high-quality product).

PASTA-MAKING BASICS

Pasta can be either fresh—with or without eggs—or dried (usually eggless, but sometimes made with eggs). Making fresh pasta is a common practice in Italian households, and trust me, it doesn't require a master's degree in culinary arts when it comes to creating a good fresh pasta. For Sunday lunch, families indulge themselves with a meal that often lasts two to three hours and during which everyone enjoys gorgeous, delicious fresh pasta.

However, don't sweat the idea of making pasta from scratch. Purchasing dry pasta is not considered inauthentic at all—Italians eat it daily. It's customary to religiously stock the pantry with several boxes of different pasta shapes, because the last thing you want to do is serve your signature ragù Bolognese with angel hair! Shudder along with me. Make sure you have the proper shapes to combine with the right sauce. Although there are not written rules about the best combinations, an edgy pasta like tortiglioni or rigatoni will go great with a meaty, chunky sauce, and a smooth, thick pasta like paccheri will marry perfectly with a fish set.

And when you have a little pasta remaining from different boxes, mix them all together to create *pasta mista*, which will work beautifully in your *pasta e fagioli* (page 133).

As I mentioned earlier, this book is not about pasta making, but I want to include my recipes for two fresh pasta doughs, one with eggs and one without. If you are gluten-free, there are many good dried pasta options on the market.

Pasta making is not a pure science and you can adjust these recipes to your taste. Experiment with shapes, textures, and cooking times. You'll find that making fresh pasta is surprisingly easy and inexpensive, and it can be a fun activity to try out in the kitchen.

PASTA SHAPES

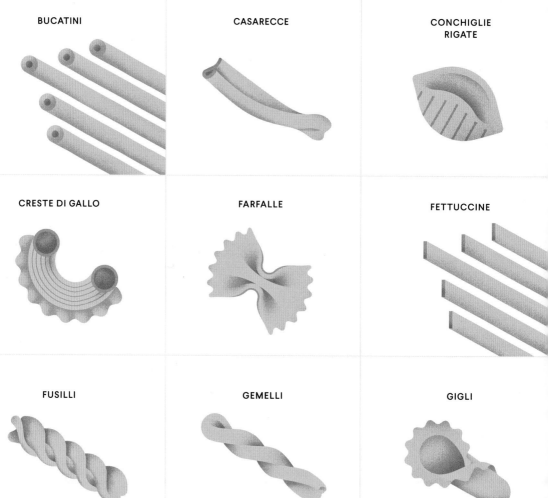

BUCATINI

CASARECCE

CONCHIGLIE RIGATE

CRESTE DI GALLO

FARFALLE

FETTUCCINE

FUSILLI

GEMELLI

GIGLI

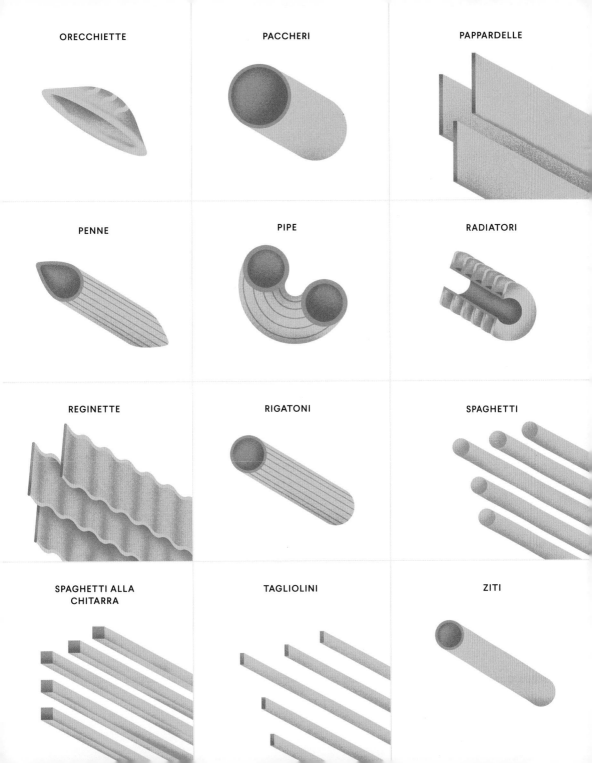

ORECCHIETTE

PACCHERI

PAPPARDELLE

PENNE

PIPE

RADIATORI

REGINETTE

RIGATONI

SPAGHETTI

SPAGHETTI ALLA
CHITARRA

TAGLIOLINI

ZITI

Pasta senza uova / **Eggless Pasta**

3½ cups durum
wheat flour
1 cup lukewarm water

This is the pasta dough recipe that I grew up with, the one that my mother uses and that both my grandmothers used. It's the classic southern Italian recipe where durum wheat flour is the star. One of my favorite durum flours is the Saragolla variety, the ancestor of modern durum wheats.

The way I have been taught is to measure the flour with your hands, using one handful of flour per guest. That means four handfuls if you have four people to serve, although five is better because you always need to be prepared to feed the potential extra guest, as my mom always says.

For the water, I never saw any of the women in my family measuring it out; their formula was to use as much as the flour needs, in order to have a dough that is not too wet and not too dry. Just pour it slowly and you will figure it out. Making pasta is about going by feel and trusting yourself. This lesson remains a fond memory of my childhood, but I can see the challenge for beginners, so here's a slightly more precise recipe. After you've made it once or twice, I suspect you won't need these instructions at all.

MAKES 4 SERVINGS

In a large mixing bowl, add the flour. Start slowly pouring in the water with one hand and mixing with the other one.

Keep kneading the flour using the heel of your hand, adding more water when necessary, aiming to have the flour absorb as much of the water as possible. Transfer the dough to a wooden cutting board or a flat surface.

Continue energetically kneading, folding, and rotating the dough. The process should take 15 to 20 minutes, depending on the power of your hand movements. At some point, the dough will transform under your hand and become elastic and silky smooth.

When you think you are done, cut the dough in half; you should not see any holes. If you see them, it means you didn't knead enough, so continue to knead.

When the dough is ready, form it into a nice round ball and cover with a clean kitchen towel (no smelly laundry detergents, please) or plastic wrap. Let it rest for 20 minutes and then proceed to roll it out and craft your desired pasta shape.

You can either use a pasta machine or a rolling pin to make the pasta sheets. In a machine, start the dough in the widest setting (usually the smallest number). Roll the dough a couple of times on that setting, dusting with a little flour as needed to prevent sticking, then move to the next setting and so on. Proceed until you obtain the desired thickness, then cut or shape the pasta. When using a rolling pin, press and fold the dough several times until you obtain the correct thickness for the desired pasta shape.

Pasta all'uovo / **Egg Pasta**

3½ cups 00 flour
4 medium good-quality
   eggs

This is a delicious and wholesome pasta dough, traditionally from northern and central Italy. Using good-quality organic, free-range eggs is the key for a great result.

MAKES 4 SERVINGS

On a clean flat surface, make a "volcano" with your flour by mounding it up and creating a well in the middle. Place the eggs in the well. With a fork or your hand, mix the eggs, pulling in some flour from the volcano walls as you mix. When the eggs and flour are completely combined, discard the fork and start using your hands.

Using the heel of your hand, energetically knead, fold, and rotate the dough. The process should take 15 to 20 minutes, depending on the power of your hand movements. At some point, the dough will transform under your hand and become elastic and silky smooth.

When you think you are done, cut the dough in half; you should not see any holes. If you see them, it means you didn't knead enough, so continue to knead.

When the dough is ready, form it into a nice round ball and cover with a clean kitchen towel (no smelly laundry detergents, please) or plastic wrap. Let it rest for 20 minutes and then proceed to roll it out and craft your desired pasta shape.

You can either use a pasta machine or a rolling pin to make the pasta sheets. In a machine, start the dough in the widest setting (usually the smallest number). Roll the dough a couple of times on that setting, dusting with a little flour as needed to prevent sticking, then move to the next setting and so on. Proceed until you obtain the desired thickness, then cut or shape the pasta. When using a rolling pin, press and fold the dough several times until you obtain the correct thickness for the desired pasta shape.

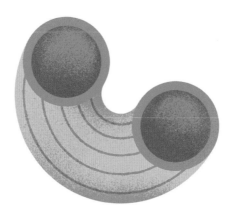

ROLLING OUT AND SHAPING PASTA

Once the dough is rested and ready, it's time to shape your pasta. There are hundreds of shapes you can craft—some easier, and others that require more technique.

If you want to make a long pasta, such as tagliatelle or pappardelle, you have the option to simply roll the dough out with a rolling pin until the sheet is about ⅛ inch thick or less. The sheet should be almost transparent; if you put your hand behind it, you should see the shadow. (Alternatively, you can use a pasta machine to make the sheets. I own an old, beautiful Marcato Atlas 150 that still works great after twenty years, despite been used a lot. Another favorite Italian-made pasta machine brand is Imperia.)

After rolling, dust a flat work surface and the dough sheet with flour, and proceed to cut it into strips: about ¼ inch wide for tagliatelle or about 1 inch for pappardelle. Separate the strips and let them dry for at least 20 minutes before cooking.

Some pasta shapes require tools to make, but others like cavatelli or orecchiette can be executed with your hands.

To make cavatelli, for instance, roll the dough into ropes about ½ inch thick, then use a knife to cut each rope into ½-inch pieces. Press and roll each piece with two fingers until you create an indentation and the pasta curls up.

Making orecchiette uses a similar process. After cutting the dough rope into pieces, you have the option to use either a butter knife or your thumb. Press and roll each piece of dough toward you and then flip it in the opposite direction to obtain a "little ear" shape.

Keep in mind that handmade pasta means handcrafted shapes, and therefore the pieces don't all need to be identical as long as they are not substantially different in size, so they can be cooked and drained at the same time.

For more information about making and shaping pasta, a few useful and gorgeous books are:

- *Pasta* by Missy Robbins
- *American Sfoglino* by Evan Funke
- *Mastering Pasta* by Marc Vetri
- *Flour + Water: Pasta* by Thomas McNaughton

Spring

Gigli con pesto di ortiche e noci, ricotta salata e olio di peperoncino calabrese / Gigli with Olympic Peninsula Stinging Nettle and Walnut Pesto, Ricotta Salata, and Calabrian Chili Oil

3 to 4 ounces young
stinging nettles
½ cup raw walnuts
½ cup extra-virgin
olive oil
½ cup grated
Parmigiano-Reggiano
Kosher salt and freshly
ground black pepper
12 ounces gigli pasta
⅓ cup grated ricotta
salata
2 tablespoons
Calabrian chili oil
8 to 10 edible spring
flowers

Ortiche—or nettles—are unquestionably a sign of spring in the Pacific Northwest. This gorgeous region has a bounty of nettles ready to be harvested usually starting in April, when the plants are still young and tender. Hiking to a secret spot to forage nettles is a quintessential local activity, although it is common to find wild nettles in the backyards of many houses on the Olympic Peninsula and surrounding areas. Searching for nettles brings back memories of when I was a young kid in Italy: I used to go foraging with my *nonna* behind the little wine cellar we had at the farm. There were so many nettles waiting to be picked, processed, and cooked in a frittata religiously made with fresh brown eggs. Here, I've developed a nettle pesto recipe that incorporates what should be a must-have seasonal condiment for anyone living in the PNW.

MAKES 4 SERVINGS

Bring a large pot of salted water to a boil. In the meantime, put on gloves and clean the nettles, removing the stems and keeping just the leaves. Rinse the leaves, then blanch them in the boiling water for less than a minute. Cool them down under cold water or in an ice bath.

Be sure to wear gloves to avoid being stung by the nettles. Blanching them is a necessary step to neutralize the stinging part.

If you have access to a good amount of nettles, you can prepare a lot of pesto in jars, and store them in the fridge for up to 5 days or freeze for a couple of months. Just make sure to cover the pesto in each jar with a drizzle of extra-virgin olive oil to prevent oxidation.

When the nettles are cool, drain them, making sure to remove the excess water. In a food processor on low speed, blend the nettles, walnuts, olive oil, and Parmigiano, until the pesto is creamy but not liquefied (it should still have some texture). Season with salt and pepper to taste.

Meanwhile, in a large pot of boiling salted water, cook the gigli until al dente and drain. In a medium pan over medium heat, quickly sauté the pasta and pesto for a minute, adding pasta water as necessary to bind the ingredients.

Plate in four bowls. Finish with the ricotta salata, a drizzle of Calabrian chili oil, and a couple of edible flowers. Enjoy the spring season on a plate.

Conchiglie rigate con cime di felce del Pacific Northwest e porro, noci, Fiore Sardo e pepe di Aleppo /
Conchiglie Rigate with Pacific Northwest Wild Fiddlehead Fern, Leek, and Walnut Pesto, Fiore Sardo, and Aleppo Pepper

2 cups fiddlehead ferns, well cleaned, dirty parts trimmed and discarded

1 leek, roots and thick green stems trimmed and discarded

½ cup raw walnuts

½ cup grated Fiore Sardo DOP, divided

⅓ cup extra-virgin olive oil

Kosher salt and freshly ground black pepper

12 ounces conchiglie rigate pasta

1 tablespoon Aleppo pepper

Fiddlehead ferns are a signal that spring has arrived, and luckily, they grow spontaneously and are widespread in PNW forests. Their color reflects their flavor—they taste like the deep, moist green of the trees, yet they carry a delicate, unique taste. Fiddlehead hunting is fun and rewarding. They are easy to recognize, even by kids, with that curled top at the end of beautiful fern leaves. Let the weather be your foraging guide: those gorgeous delicacies can grow up to six inches overnight after a warm spring rain!

MAKES 4 SERVINGS

In a large pot of boiling salted water, blanch the fiddleheads for 5 minutes. Leave the water boiling, and use a slotted spoon or spider to remove the fiddleheads. Rinse them with cold water, and set aside, reserving about a dozen for finishing.

In the same pot, blanch the leek for 2 minutes and set aside.

When both fiddleheads and leek are cool, in a food processor, blend the fiddleheads, leek, walnuts, half the Fiore Sardo, and the olive oil until creamy like a puree. If the result is too thick, add water until you have the desired consistency. Season with salt and pepper to taste.

Return the water in the same pot to a boil, then cook the conchiglie rigate until al dente and drain. In a medium-large pan over medium heat, quickly sauté the pasta and pesto, adding pasta water as necessary to bind the ingredients. Add 2 tablespoons of the Fiore Sardo, and stir to combine.

Plate in four bowls. Finish with the reserved fiddleheads, the remaining ¼ cup Fiore Sardo, the Aleppo pepper, and a drizzle of oil.

Penne con pancetta, piselli, porro e crème fraîche / **Penne with Pancetta, Sweet Peas, Leeks, and Crème Fraîche**

¼ cup extra-virgin olive oil

3 ounces pancetta, cut into ½-inch cubes

1 medium leek, thinly sliced, roots and thick green stems trimmed and discarded

2 Yukon Gold potatoes, cut into ½-inch cubes

1 bunch thyme, stemmed

14 ounces fresh English peas

Kosher salt and freshly ground black pepper

12 ounces penne pasta

⅓ cup grated Parmigiano-Reggiano

¼ cup crème fraîche

This is an incredibly easy and fast recipe inspired by the French soup vichyssoise. It's ideal for the spring months when fresh peas are available, but you can substitute frozen ones for an affordable, delicious, and year-round pasta dish. Additionally, you can use bacon instead of the pancetta, and the crème fraîche can be replaced with fresh ricotta.

MAKES 4 SERVINGS

In a medium-large skillet over medium heat, warm the olive oil. Add the pancetta and sauté until it becomes crispy, stirring to avoid burning.

Add the leek and the potatoes, and cook until firm but soft enough to put a fork through. Stir in the thyme. Add the peas and cook, stirring occasionally, for 5 to 6 minutes. Season with salt and pepper to taste. Turn off the heat, but leave the pan on the burner.

Meanwhile, in a large pot of boiling salted water, cook the penne until al dente, drain, and transfer to the skillet. Add the Parmigiano and quickly sauté, adding pasta water as necessary to bind the ingredients.

Plate in four bowls. Finish with a spoonful of crème fraîche, a drizzle of oil, more pepper, and a thyme sprig for decoration.

Radiatori con pesto di germogli di pisello, pistacchi, pecorino e olio di jalapeño / **Radiatori with Pea Shoot and Pistachio Pesto, Pecorino, and Jalapeño Chili Oil**

4 cups pea shoots
⅓ cup grated pecorino
¼ cup shelled pistachios
Juice of 1 medium lemon
⅓ cup extra-virgin olive oil
Kosher salt and freshly ground black pepper
12 ounces radiatori pasta
1 tablespoon jalapeño chili oil (recipe follows)

Sweet and grassy at the same time, pea shoots are cultivated in the PNW and are ready to be harvested in the late spring. With their delicious tendrils, they are perfect in a salad and can also be used in a delicate pesto for a spring vegetarian pasta dish.

MAKES 4 SERVINGS

In a food processor, pulse the pea shoots (reserving a few shoots for finishing), pecorino, pistachios, and lemon juice, adding the olive oil slowly until you obtain a creamy consistency. Season with salt and pepper to taste. In a medium pan over low heat, warm the pesto.

Meanwhile, in a large pot of boiling salted water, cook the radiatori until al dente, drain, and transfer to the pan. Quickly sauté, adding pasta water as necessary to bind the ingredients.

Plate in four bowls. Finish with pecorino, the reserved pea shoots, and a nice drizzle of jalapeño chili oil.

1 cup extra-virgin
   olive oil
2 whole dry jalapeño
   peppers, stemmed

JALAPEÑO CHILI OIL

There are many ways to make a spicy extra-virgin olive oil. The easiest and safest one is to use dry peppers.

MAKES 1 CUP

In a big pot of boiling water, place a bottle, and let it boil for about 20 minutes. Remove the sterilized bottle from the pot and let it dry.

Put the jalapeños in the bottom of the bottle, add your favorite extra-virgin olive oil, seal the bottle, and let it rest in a dry, dark place for about a month for best flavor. The oil will keep for several months.

Ziti con pesto di spinaci e mandorle, Beecher's Flagship e cayenne africano / **Ziti with Baby Spinach, Almond, and Beecher's Flagship Pesto and African Cayenne**

½ pound fresh baby spinach, plus a few leaves for garnish

2 ounces whole raw almonds

½ cup crumbled Beecher's Flagship cheese

⅓ cup extra-virgin olive oil

¼ cup water

Kosher salt and freshly ground black pepper

12 ounces ziti pasta

Pinch of African cayenne

Tips:

Make the spinach pesto ahead of time and keep it in a container in the refrigerator for 3 to 4 days. Drizzle some extra-virgin olive oil on top to avoid oxidation.

You can substitute Beecher's Flagship cheese with another cheddar or robust semi-hard cow's milk cheese.

I have been in love with spinach in all its versions since I was a child, most likely because of my fascination with *Braccio di Ferro*, Popeye the Sailor Man. This dish highlights my lifelong obsession with spinach. While the recipe can be made year-round, fresh spinach can be found in the PNW during the warmer months of spring and summer. For those of you who love Pike Place Market (and really, who doesn't?), this pesto can be made entirely from market ingredients. Beecher's Flagship cheese does its part with its peculiar robust, nutty flavor, and the African cayenne adds a bit of spice (thanks to World Spice Merchants, a mecca for local and visiting spice lovers).

MAKES 4 SERVINGS

In a blender, blend the spinach, almonds, cheese, olive oil, water, and salt and pepper to taste, taking care not to liquefy (the pesto should still have some texture).

In a medium-large pan over medium heat, warm the pesto for a couple of minutes.

Meanwhile, in a large pot of boiling salted water, cook the ziti until al dente, drain, and transfer to the pan with the pesto. Quickly sauté for a minute, adding pasta water as necessary to bind the ingredients.

Plate in four bowls. Finish with more cheese, a pinch of cayenne, a few fresh spinach leaves, and a drizzle of oil.

Pipe con spugnole, pancetta, noci, ricotta e zafferano / Pipe with Pacific Northwest Morels, Pancetta, Walnuts, Ricotta, and Saffron

5 tablespoons extra-virgin olive oil

1 small shallot, finely chopped

2 cloves garlic, gently crushed

2 ounces pancetta, cut into ½-inch cubes

½ cup walnuts

8 ounces fresh morels, halved lengthwise

1 tablespoon finely chopped Italian parsley

½ teaspoon saffron threads, soaked in ⅓ cup boiling water for 30 minutes

Kosher salt and freshly ground black pepper

12 ounces pipe pasta

½ cup fresh cow ricotta

½ cup grated Parmigiano-Reggiano

One of the most foraged (and desirable) items in the PNW, morels can be found from mid-April until June in the woods of the Olympic Peninsula, the Okanogan-Wenatchee National Forest, the San Juan Islands, and a host of other secret spots across Washington State and Oregon.

Spugnole (or spongy ones) in Italian, morels represent the new season that is about to start: spring. This recipe uses a classic Italian combo—parsley, walnuts, pancetta, and saffron. Fresh cow ricotta is added at the end, offering a great alternative to a cream- or butter-based sauce. The result is a seasonal, luscious pasta dish that showcases the morel mushrooms with their nutty and earthy flavor and is perfectly balanced with the other ingredients.

MAKES 4 SERVINGS

In a large pan over medium heat, warm the olive oil. Add the shallot and garlic and sauté for 2 minutes, stirring to avoid burning. Add the pancetta and walnuts, and cook for 2 minutes, stirring with a wooden spoon.

Add the morels and continue cooking for 1 minute. Add the parsley, saffron water, and salt and pepper to taste, and continue cooking for another 2 minutes. Turn off the heat, but leave the pan on the burner.

→

Meanwhile, in a large pot of boiling salted water, cook the pipe until al dente, drain, and transfer to the pan. Energetically stir in the ricotta, making sure the pasta is blended. Add two-thirds of the Parmigiano, and stir to combine.

Plate in four bowls. Finish with additional walnuts, the remaining Parmigiano, and a drizzle of oil.

How to clean mushrooms

Mushrooms need to be cleaned right before using them. The general rule is to handle them as little as possible, since they are delicate gifts from nature. Shake the mushrooms to get rid of loose dirt. Use a mushroom brush or damp cloth to remove soil residue. Soak morels in cold water for 2 to 3 minutes, rinse, and repeat twice (or more if necessary), then dry with a clean kitchen towel or paper towel. Uncleaned mushrooms will keep in the refrigerator for a few days in a paper bag with some holes poked in it.

Pipe con gamberi del Pacific Northwest, asparagi viola e limone / **Pipe with Pacific Northwest Spot Prawns, Purple Asparagus, and Lemon**

1 pound purple or green asparagus, trimmed, tips and stems separated

4 tablespoons extra-virgin olive oil, divided

2 cloves garlic, gently crushed

1 pound fresh wild spot prawns, washed, peeled, and heads removed

¼ teaspoon cayenne powder

Kosher salt and freshly ground black pepper

12 ounces pipe pasta

Zest from 1 medium lemon

Two ingredients announce the arrival of spring in the PNW: spot prawns and asparagus. Pacific Northwesterners impatiently wait for the spot prawn season, which usually starts in May and runs through the end of September. Those sweet sea creatures, with their distinctive briny and buttery flavor, can be found from the Salish Sea to Hood Canal.

Then there's asparagus. Asparagus is grown in Washington State over almost five thousand acres, which makes Washington the nation's top producer. Harvested primarily from April through June in the Columbia Valley, asparagus is among my favorite vegetables for its crunchiness and unique taste.

MAKES 4 SERVINGS

In a medium pot of boiling water, blanch the asparagus stems for 5 minutes, then drain. In a food processor, blend the asparagus stems and 1 tablespoon of the olive oil until you obtain a creamy consistency. Set aside.

In a medium-large skillet over medium heat, warm the remaining 3 tablespoons olive oil. Add the garlic and sauté for a couple of minutes, stirring to avoid burning.

$\rightarrow$

Don't throw away the spot prawn heads; use them for a delicious stock or broth.

When zesting a lemon, take care to only grate the yellow peel and avoid the bitter white pith below.

Increase the heat to medium-high, stir in the spot prawns and asparagus tips, and cook, stirring occasionally, for 3 to 4 minutes, until the spot prawns turn pink. Add the cayenne and salt and pepper to taste, and stir. Turn off the heat, but leave the pan on the burner.

Meanwhile, in a large pot of boiling salted water, cook the pipe until al dente, drain, and transfer to the skillet. Quickly stir in the blended asparagus stems.

Plate in four bowls. Finish with the lemon zest and a drizzle of oil, and enjoy.

Tagliolini con halibut fresco, asparagi, mandorle e sommacco / **Tagliolini with Halibut, Asparagus, Almonds, and Sumac**

3 tablespoons extra-virgin olive oil

½ small shallot, finely minced

12 ounces asparagus, stems cut into 1-inch pieces and tips set aside

¼ cup toasted almonds, crushed

¼ teaspoon dried oregano

Pinch of red pepper flakes

Kosher salt and freshly ground black pepper

10 ounces fresh halibut fillet, cut into 1-inch strips

12 ounces tagliolini pasta

1 teaspoon sumac

Native to the northern Pacific Ocean, these gorgeous diamond-shaped fish are extensively caught from March until November. In my mind, halibut qualifies as a spring delicacy when it first appears on fish market counters, although it is available for several months. Popular for its gentle and mild flavor, halibut is best cooked lightly because it can go from flaky and delicious to tough if overcooked. I grew up eating it occasionally in Italy, where it is considered a special treat since it's not native to Italian waters. Seeing halibut so fresh and available in the PNW is a joy. This recipe uses tagliolini pasta and goes for a classic combination of halibut and asparagus. Add to that some crunchiness from the almonds and a little kick from the sumac and you've got a stunner of a dish.

MAKES 4 SERVINGS

In a medium-large skillet over medium heat, warm the olive oil. Add the shallot and sauté for 2 to 3 minutes.

Add the asparagus stems, almonds, oregano, red pepper flakes, and salt and pepper to taste, reduce the heat to medium-low, and cook, covered, for 5 to 6 minutes, or until thick and saucy.

Uncover, increase the heat to medium, add the halibut and asparagus tips, and cook for 2 to 3 minutes, flipping a few times but being careful not to shred the halibut.

Meanwhile, in a large pot of boiling salted water, cook the tagliolini until al dente, drain, and transfer to the skillet. Quickly sauté for a minute, adding pasta water as necessary to bind the ingredients.

Plate in four bowls. Top with more crushed almonds, the sumac, and a drizzle of oil.

Reginette con sugo di agnello di Lopez Island / **Reginette with Lopez Island Lamb Sugo**

6 tablespoons extra-virgin olive oil

½ medium white onion, diced

2 carrots, cut into 1-inch rounds

½ pound lamb shoulder, cut into 1-inch cubes

2 lamb ribs

3 to 4 bay leaves

⅓ cup dry red wine

32 ounces (4 cups) canned San Marzano tomato puree

Kosher salt and freshly ground black pepper

12 ounces reginette pasta

3 knobs unsalted butter

¼ cup grated pecorino

Lamb meat can be found on many Italian tables, especially around Easter, and it can take different forms. Here is a classic *sugo di agnello* made with 100-percent grass-raised lambs from Lopez Island. Lopez, and other islands in the San Juans, has a tradition of natural farming without sprays, chemicals, or fertilized grass. Stonecrest Farm & Graziers is a great example of responsible farming: baby lambs are raised and nurtured by their mothers, running and playing on the hills overlooking the island's central valley.

MAKES 4 SERVINGS

In a medium saucepan over medium-low heat, warm the olive oil. Add the onions and carrots; sauté for 2 to 3 minutes.

Increase the heat to medium, add the lamb shoulder and ribs and the bay leaves, and cook, stirring occasionally, for 4 to 5 minutes. Add the wine and continue cooking for 2 to 3 minutes, or until the alcohol evaporates.

Reduce the heat to low, stir in the tomato puree, season with salt and pepper to taste, and cook, stirring occasionally, for 45 to 60 minutes, or until the sauce has a dense consistency.

Meanwhile, in a large pot of boiling salted water, cook the reginette until al dente, drain, and transfer to a large mixing bowl. Add half the lamb sauce and the butter, stir, then add the pecorino and stir until the butter is melted.

Plate in four bowls and finish with a scoop of the sauce, more pecorino, and a drizzle of oil. Enjoy with a glass of full-bodied red wine.

Paccheri con polpo gigante del Pacific Northwest, patate, olive Gaeta e capperi /
Paccheri with Giant Pacific Octopus, Potatoes, Gaeta Olives, and Capers

1 pound giant Pacific octopus tentacle, rinsed until clean (see Tip)

3 tablespoons extra-virgin olive oil

1 small shallot, finely chopped

2 small Yukon Gold potatoes, cut into ½-inch cubes

12 to 15 Gaeta or Castelvetrano olives, pitted and halved

1 bunch Italian parsley, minced, divided

1 tablespoon brined capers, drained

¼ teaspoon dried oregano

Pinch of red pepper flakes

Kosher salt and freshly ground black pepper

6 to 7 cherry tomatoes, halved (optional)

12 ounces paccheri pasta

Giant Pacific octopi are beautiful local creatures able to grow up to 150 pounds, although their average weight is closer to 50. They are delicious; I love the slow, low-temperature oven cooking that makes their tentacles soft and juicy. Classic Italian ingredients like Gaeta or Castelvetrano olives, capers, and parsley pair perfectly with it. Without overshadowing the octopus, they bring out its flavor and texture, allowing it to really shine. And the shape of paccheri is simply heavenly for this recipe.

MAKES 4 SERVINGS

Preheat the oven to 180 degrees F.

On a baking sheet, place the octopus, cover it with foil, and bake for about 2 hours, draining every 20 to 30 minutes to prevent it from boiling in its own juices. Reserve the juices to use in future recipes or toss it.

Once the octopus is soft and fork-tender, let it cool down—it will be easier to cut without it breaking apart. When cool enough to handle, cut the tentacles in ½-inch rounds.

Tip: It's possible to buy the octopus already cleaned at the fish market, but in case it's not, scrub the tentacles with a kitchen brush and rinse them under cold running water, making sure all possible grit is gone.

In a medium-large sauté pan over medium heat, warm the olive oil for a minute. Add the shallot and sauté for about 1 minute, or until softened. Add the potatoes and cook, stirring, for 3 to 4 minutes. Add the olives, half the parsley, the capers, oregano, and red pepper flakes. Reduce the heat to medium-low, and cook for 2 minutes. Add the octopus and gently stir. Season with salt and pepper to taste. Add the tomatoes, reduce the heat to low, and cover with a lid. Continue cooking for 3 to 4 minutes, or until the tomatoes are breaking down and creating some juice.

Meanwhile, in a large pot of boiling salted water, cook the paccheri until al dente, drain, and transfer to the sauté pan. Quickly sauté, adding pasta water as necessary to bind the ingredients.

Plate in four bowls. Finish with the remaining parsley, some black pepper, and a drizzle of oil.

Pipe con radicchio, pancetta, noci e gorgonzola dolce / **Pipe with Spring Radicchio, Pancetta, Walnuts, and Gorgonzola Dolce**

2 tablespoons extra-virgin olive oil

3 ounces pancetta, cut into ½-inch cubes

½ cup walnuts halves, gently crushed

1 pound Trevisano radicchio, cut into thin strips

½ pound Gorgonzola Dolce, shredded

Kosher salt and freshly ground black pepper

12 ounces pipe pasta

½ cup grated Parmigiano-Reggiano

I simply had to include radicchio in this book. This bittersweet beauty, which has its roots in Italy's Veneto region, can be found in a hundred recipes back home, both cooked and raw. PNW farmers love to grow radicchio, and it's always a joy to discover it at the farmers' market in the spring.

The following recipe features the classic pairing of walnuts and Gorgonzola Dolce: you cannot go wrong with it. The pancetta makes things better because . . . pancetta.

I have to give a shout-out to my dear friend Lucio Gomiero, winemaker of great Vignalta wines on the Italian Euganean Hills, who for fun started to introduce radicchio in the United States. His Salinas-based firm became the world's largest producer in the '80s with Trevisano, Chioggia, and Castelvetrano varieties. Here is my tribute to this visionary, humble human being and extraordinary cook.

MAKES 4 SERVINGS

In a medium-large sauté pan over medium-low heat, warm the olive oil for 1 minute. Add the pancetta and walnuts, and sauté until the pancetta becomes crispy, 2 to 3 minutes.

Add two-thirds of the radicchio and sauté, stirring occasionally, for 3 to 4 minutes.

Reduce the heat to low, add the Gorgonzola Dolce, stirring, and allow it to melt almost completely. Season with salt and pepper to taste.

Meanwhile, in a large pot of boiling salted water, cook the pipe until al dente, drain, and transfer to the sauté pan. Quickly sauté for a minute, adding pasta water as necessary to bind the ingredients.

Plate in four bowls. Finish with the Parmigiano and the remaining radicchio.

Ziti con salmone selvaggio argentato, fave e menta / **Ziti with Wild Coho Salmon, Fava Beans, and Mint**

3 tablespoons extra-virgin olive oil

1 small shallot, finely chopped

8 to 10 leaves spearmint, finely chopped, plus 4 whole leaves for finishing

1 sprig wild fennel, minced

1 pound fresh fava beans, shelled

⅓ cup water

Kosher salt and freshly ground black pepper

12 ounces wild coho salmon, shredded into small pieces

12 ounces ziti pasta

As summer approaches, the sun shines brightly and our palate desires nothing but the freshest ingredients, so here is a recipe that positively bursts with seasonal flavors. Wild coho salmon are well known to fishermen as "silvers" thanks to their gorgeous pearly color and are a quintessential summer catch in the Pacific Northwest. Mild and delicate, the fish fuses wonderfully with several seasonal greens, but I have to admit that the coho-fava-mint combination makes this a superb culinary ménage à trois.

MAKES 4 SERVINGS

In a medium-large pan over medium-low heat, warm the olive oil for 1 minute. Add the shallot, mint, and wild fennel, and sauté for 2 minutes.

Stir in the fava beans and cook for a minute. Add the water and cook for another 3 to 4 minutes. Season with salt and pepper to taste. Turn off the heat.

In a blender or food processer, blend half the fava bean mixture until you obtain a creamy consistency. Set aside.

Turn the heat back on to medium, and add the salmon to the remaining fava bean mixture. Cook for 2 to 3 minutes, stirring occasionally.

Meanwhile, in a large pot of boiling salted water, cook the ziti until al dente, drain, and transfer to the pan along with the creamy fava bean mixture. Quickly sauté for a minute, adding pasta water as necessary to bind the ingredients.

Plate in four bowls. Finish with a whole spearmint leaf and a drizzle of oil, then serve.

Summer

Pappardelle con fegatini di pollo alla veneziana e peperoncini Mama Lil's / **Pappardelle with Venetian-Style Chicken Liver and Mama Lil's Spicy Peppers**

¼ cup extra-virgin olive oil

2 tablespoons unsalted butter

2 medium white onions, cut into ¼-inch strips

8 sage leaves, finely chopped

Pinch of red pepper flakes

½ cup water

1 tablespoon apple cider vinegar

1 pound organic, free-range chicken liver, rinsed and cut into ¼-inch strips

Kosher salt and freshly ground black pepper

12 ounces pappardelle pasta

⅓ cup grated Parmigiano-Reggiano, divided

¼ cup Mama Lil's spicy peppers, or pickled red onions (page 56)

Fegato alla veneziana is a traditional Italian *secondo piatto* originally from Venice but served all over Italy. It was one of my favorite meat dishes growing up and my mom served a lot of it during my childhood under my pediatrician's advice to add more iron in my diet.

This is a reinterpretation of the recipe, pasta being an unheard-of ingredient in the dish in Italy. I have substituted veal liver, which is harder to find, with the more common chicken liver, which is also milder. This dish is for everyone who loves liver and doesn't get to see it often on the menu. It has been a hit at my restaurant.

MAKES 4 SERVINGS

In a medium-large skillet over medium heat, warm the olive oil and butter for a couple of minutes.

Add the onions, sage, and red pepper flakes, and sauté for 2 to 4 minutes. Add the water and vinegar, reduce the heat to medium-low, and cook for 5 minutes.

Increase the heat to medium, add the liver, and cook for another 5 to 7 minutes, or until the sauce is not too loose and watery. Season with salt and pepper to taste. Turn off the heat, but leave the pan on the burner.

Be careful not to over-cook the liver; other-wise, it will become extremely hard.

I often make this recipe with pickled red onions instead of Mama Lil's peppers, which is a great alternative.

Meanwhile, in a large pot of boiling salted water, cook the pappardelle until al dente, drain, and transfer the pasta and ¼ cup of the Parmigiano to the skillet. Quickly sauté the pasta, adding pasta water as necessary to bind the ingredients.

Plate in four bowls. Finish with the remaining Parmigiano, a drizzle of oil, and a few Mama Lil's spicy peppers. Enjoy!

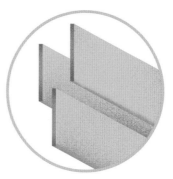

Fusilli con purè di cipolle Walla Walla, noci, formaggio Twin Sisters Farmhouse e cipolla rossa sottaceto / **Fusilli with Walla Walla Sweet Onion and Walnut Puree, Twin Sisters Farmhouse with Whole Peppercorn Cheese, and Pickled Red Onions**

2 Walla Walla sweet onions, halved
Kosher salt and freshly ground black pepper
½ cup water
⅓ cup extra-virgin olive oil, divided
2 ounces whole walnuts
½ cup grated Parmigiano-Reggiano
12 ounces fusilli pasta
⅓ cup grated Twin Sisters Creamery's Farmhouse with Whole Peppercorns
¼ cup pickled red onions (recipe follows), or 8 Mama Lil's spicy peppers (see Tip)

This recipe offers multiple tributes to Washington State. Stunning Walla Walla County is represented by its large sweet onions. When I had Walla Walla sweet onions for the first time, I was surprised by their mild, juicy flavor. The round shape made me want to bite into them raw! This PNW ingredient marks the beginning of summer; the harvest usually starts in mid-June. Travel next to the Twin Sisters Creamery, located in Ferndale, in the northwest corner of the state, just south of the Canadian border near the Nooksack River. There, they produce their Farmhouse with Whole Peppercorns, one of the best artisan cheeses I have discovered in Washington. These local ingredients come together and shine in this celebration of a PNW summer.

MAKES 4 SERVINGS

Preheat the oven to 350 degrees F. On a deep-rimmed baking sheet, place the onion halves, season with salt and pepper to taste, and cover with the water. Drizzle with half the olive oil, cover with aluminum foil, and bake for 45 minutes. Transfer the onions and the cooking liquid to a container. Let cool for a few hours.

Tip: If you want to
include yet another
PNW ingredient, from
the Yakima Valley, use
Mama Lil's goathorn
peppers in place of
the pickled red onions.
Be sure to drizzle the
pasta with a little of
the spicy marinating
oil before serving.

In a food processor, blend the onions with liquid, the remaining olive oil, walnuts, and Parmigiano until you have a creamy puree. Take care not to liquefy the sauce.

Meanwhile, in a large pot of boiling salted water, cook the fusilli until al dente, drain, and transfer to a mixing bowl. Add the onion puree and mix well, adding pasta water as necessary to bind the ingredients.

Plate in four bowls. Finish with the farmhouse cheese and pickled red onions. Enjoy!

1 large red onion
½ cup apple cider
    vinegar
½ cup water
1 tablespoon sugar
1 teaspoon kosher salt
½ teaspoon black
    peppercorns
½ teaspoon mustard
    seeds
1 jalapeño, halved
    lengthwise and seeds
    removed
3 cloves garlic
3 to 4 bay leaves

PICKLED RED ONIONS

MAKES ABOUT 1 CUP

Ideally with a mandolin but a sharp knife will work too, slice the red onion into thin strips. Transfer to a pint jar or small container.

In a small pot over medium heat, combine all the remaining ingredients, stir, and simmer for 4 to 5 minutes.

Pour the mixture over the onions in the jar, making sure the onions are covered to the top. Let it rest for at least 4 to 6 hours before serving.

≋

Farfalle con salmone sockeye del Pacific Northwest, carciofi marinati e capperi fritti /
Farfalle with Wild Pacific Northwest Sockeye Salmon, Marinated Artichokes, and Fried Capers

⅓ cup canola oil
1 tablespoon brined capers, drained
Kosher salt
6 tablespoons extra-virgin olive oil
1 bunch green onion, finely chopped
4 ounces marinated artichoke hearts, drained and cut into strips
10 ounces wild sockeye salmon fillet
12 ounces farfalle pasta
Ground white pepper

Tip: A store-bought jar of well-prepared artisanal lemon-marinated artichoke hearts will do the job. You can also make your own ahead of time during the summer season when artichokes are ready to be picked in the PNW.

Gorgeous with bright-orange flesh, sockeye salmon are native to the western coast of North America and pair well with several vegetables and lemony flavors. I adore cooking them with artichokes, capers, and pasta. The combination of these ingredients—artichokes are full of antioxidants and the salmon is rich in omega-3 fatty acids—makes this dish a joy for *il nostro corpo e la nostra mente*, our body and soul.

MAKES 4 SERVINGS

In a small sauté pan over high heat, warm the canola oil. When the oil is hot, add the capers and fry for 2 to 3 minutes. Scoop them out onto a paper towel to drain. Sprinkle with a pinch or two of salt and set aside.

In a large skillet over medium heat, warm the olive oil. Add the green onion and sauté for a minute, stirring to avoid burning, then add the artichokes and sauté for 2 minutes more. Add the salmon and cook, flipping occasionally, for a couple more minutes. Season with salt and pepper to taste.

Meanwhile, in a large pot of boiling salted water, cook the farfalle until al dente, drain, and transfer to the skillet. Combine the pasta with the salmon and artichokes, increase the heat to medium-high, and sauté for a minute, adding pasta water as necessary to bind the ingredients.

Plate in four bowls. Finish with the capers, a drizzle of olive oil, and some white pepper.

Paccheri con tonno alalunga fresco, melanzane, capperi e menta / **Paccheri with Wild Pacific Northwest Albacore Tuna, Eggplant, Capers, and Mint**

1 medium zucchini, cut into ½-inch rounds

Pinch of red pepper flakes

Kosher salt and freshly ground black pepper

¼ cup extra-virgin olive oil

1 small shallot, finely chopped

2 cloves garlic, gently crushed

8 to 10 spearmint leaves, finely chopped

1 tablespoon brined capers, drained

1 small eggplant, cut into 2-inch cubes

4 ounces albacore tuna fillet

12 ounces paccheri pasta

1 teaspoon dried oregano

Cherry tomatoes, halved, for garnish (optional)

Every summer I wait impatiently for the arrival of the tuna-fishing season, so I can make this traditional Italian pasta dish that incorporates the classic Sicilian combo of eggplant, mint, and capers.

North Pacific albacore tuna are typically fished between July and September by troller boats off the Washington State coastline. The taste of fresh-caught albacore, with its firm, steak-like texture, is a delight for any palate, and I'm transported straight to the southern coast of Italy every time I make this recipe.

MAKES 4 SERVINGS

In a large pot of boiling salted water, blanch the zucchini for 5 minutes, drain, and put in a food processor with the red pepper flakes, a pinch of salt and pepper, and 2 tablespoons of the olive oil. Blend until creamy and set aside.

In a large pan over medium heat, warm the remaining 2 tablespoons olive oil. Add the shallot, garlic, three-quarters of the mint, and the capers, and sauté for 1 minute. Stir in the eggplant so that all the pieces are coated with olive oil. Season with salt and pepper to taste, cover, and reduce the heat to medium-low. Cook for 3 to 4 minutes, then uncover, increase the heat to medium, stir in the tuna, and cook for 1 minute.

Meanwhile, in a large pot of boiling salted water, cook the paccheri until al dente, drain, and transfer to the pan. Add the zucchini sauce and oregano and sauté for 1 minute, adding pasta water as necessary to bind the ingredients.

Plate in four bowls, top with the remaining mint, and serve.

Ziti con pesto di rucola, zenzero e noci, ricotta salata e olio di peperoncino habanero / Ziti with Arugula, Ginger, and Walnut Pesto, Ricotta Salata, and Red Habanero Chili Oil

4 cups baby arugula

½ cup raw walnuts

½ cup grated pecorino or Parmigiano-Reggiano

½ cup extra-virgin olive oil

1 small Yukon Gold or other potato variety, boiled and cooled

1 ounce fresh ginger, grated

Kosher salt and freshly ground black pepper

12 ounces ziti pasta

⅓ cup grated ricotta salata

2 tablespoons red habanero chili oil

Tip: Habanero chili oil can be swapped out for another spicy oil.

Rucola, or arugula, is an easy vegetable to grow in this region. It germinates fast, grows even faster, and has many uses in the kitchen. I love arugula mixed with ginger for a bitter yet spicy taste, and it can be toned down by blending in a boiled-and-cooled potato. Arugula was probably an overused ingredient in the '80s and '90s in Italy—it sounded very "modern" to add it everywhere and anywhere, like on top of pasta or pizza—but it never lost its appeal. When I think of *rucola,* my mind goes to the wild variety that grows spontaneously in the field—it's made of darker, thinner leaves, and is incredibly pungent. During my childhood, I was told to go and pick it, so we could add a few of its bitter leaves to a salad or panino.

MAKES 4 SERVINGS

In a blender on the lowest speed, blend the arugula, walnuts, pecorino, olive oil, potato, and ginger, until combined but not liquefied (the pesto should still have some texture). Season with salt and pepper to taste.

Meanwhile, in a large pot of boiling salted water, cook the ziti until al dente, drain, and transfer to a mixing bowl with the pesto. Energetically stir the pasta and sauce, adding pasta water as necessary to bind the ingredients.

Plate in four bowls. Add the ricotta salata, some habanero chili oil, and a few arugula leaves on top. Enjoy!

Fusilli con zucchine, limone, menta, mandorle tostate e fiori di zucca fritti /
Fusilli with Zucchini, Lemon, Mint, Toasted Almonds, and Fried Zucchini Blossoms

¼ cup extra-virgin olive oil

1 clove garlic, gently crushed

1 pound zucchini, cut into ½-inch cubes

Kosher salt and freshly ground black pepper

7 to 8 spearmint leaves, finely chopped

Zest of 1 medium organic lemon

12 ounces fusilli pasta

⅓ cup grated Parmigiano-Reggiano

⅓ cup crushed toasted almonds

8 to 12 fried zucchini blossoms (recipe follows)

Zucchini, lemons, mint, almonds, and zucchini blossoms—all ingredients reminiscent of summer. Zucchini and their blossoms absolutely explode off the vine in Seattle neighborhoods and community gardens during the summer months. In raised boxes, front yards, P-Patches, and parking strips, they are everywhere. And it's no wonder: it's one of the easiest veggies to grow in the PNW, and this recipe makes great use of them.

MAKES 4 SERVINGS

In a medium-large skillet over medium heat, warm the olive oil. Add the garlic and sauté for 1 minute, stirring to avoid burning.

Add the zucchini, and cook, stirring occasionally, for 3 to 4 minutes.

Season with salt and pepper to taste, add the mint and lemon zest, and cook for another 2 minutes. Turn off the heat, but leave the pan on the burner.

Meanwhile, in a large pot of boiling salted water, cook the fusilli until al dente, drain, and transfer to the skillet. Add the Parmigiano and sauté quickly for a minute, adding pasta water as necessary to bind the ingredients.

Plate in four bowls and finish with the almonds and zucchini blossoms. Enjoy such a fresh summer pasta dish with a cold glass of white wine.

¾ cup all-purpose flour
1 teaspoon baking soda
Kosher salt
¾ cup water
1 cup vegetable oil
8 to 10 zucchini
   blossoms

FRIED ZUCCHINI BLOSSOMS

This is the traditional way we fry zucchini blossoms in Italy: by dipping them in *pastella*, a simple yet delicious coating.

In a mixing bowl, whisk together the flour, baking soda, and salt. Slowly add the water, stirring, until you obtain a smooth, runny consistency.

In a skillet over medium heat, warm the vegetable oil. Test the oil by dropping in a bit of the *pastella*. If it starts bubbling, it's ready. Dip the zucchini blossom into the *pastella*, thoroughly coating, and fry each for a minute or so, flipping them halfway through, until golden brown and crispy. Remove with a spider or slotted spoon, and place on a paper towel to absorb the excess oil.

Creste di gallo con crema di peperone giallo, ricotta salata, friggitelli e pepe di Aleppo / **Creste di Gallo with Yellow Bell Pepper Puree, Ricotta Salata, Shishito Peppers, and Aleppo Pepper**

4 tablespoons extra-virgin olive oil

½ white onion, thinly sliced

3 medium yellow peppers, trimmed and cut into 1-inch strips

¼ teaspoon dried oregano

Kosher salt and freshly ground black pepper

½ cup water

12 ounces creste di gallo pasta

⅓ cup grated Parmigiano

6 ounces ricotta salata, shaved

Fried shishito peppers (recipe follows)

1 teaspoon Aleppo pepper

This dish could be called *three peppers on a plate.* It's a delightful pasta dish for the palate *and* the eyes, with the bright yellow of the bell peppers, the crunchiness of the fried shishito peppers, and the rich burgundy color of the Aleppo pepper. Inspired by *peperonata* (a classic Italian summer onion-and-pepper stew that my aunt Grazia used to make all the time), this pasta is seasonal, gorgeous, and easy.

MAKES 4 SERVINGS

In a medium saucepan over medium heat, warm the olive oil. Add the onions and sauté for 1 minute, then add the bell peppers and cook for 2 to 3 minutes. Add the oregano, season with salt and pepper to taste, and stir.

Add the water, and cover. Let the bell peppers cook for about 10 minutes, or until soft. Turn off the heat. Using an immersion blender, blend until the consistency is creamy but not liquid.

Meanwhile, in a large pot of boiling salted water, cook the creste di gallo until al dente, drain, and transfer to the saucepan. Return the heat to medium, add the Parmigiano, and combine, adding pasta water as necessary to bind the ingredients.

Plate in four bowls. Finish with the ricotta salata, shishito peppers, Aleppo pepper, and a drizzle of oil. *Buon appetito!*

⅓ cup canola oil
12 shishito peppers
Kosher salt

FRIED SHISHITO PEPPERS

MAKES 12 FRIED PEPPERS

In a medium pan over medium heat, warm the canola oil until it is shimmering hot. Add the shishito peppers, and fry them on both sides until they are brown but not burned.

Using a spider or a slotted spoon, remove the peppers and place them on paper towels to absorb the excess oil.

Sprinkle with the salt.

Casarecce con granchio del Pacific Northwest, asparagi e zenzero /
Casarecce with Pacific Northwest Crab, Asparagus, and Ginger

4 to 5 asparagus, trimmed and cut into 1-inch pieces

5 tablespoons extra-virgin olive oil

1 tablespoon salted butter

1 bunch green onions, finely chopped

½ pound cooked crabmeat

¼ cup dry white wine

1 teaspoon grated ginger

Kosher salt and freshly ground black pepper

12 ounces casarecce pasta

Dungeness, king, red rock, shore, and box are the most common crab varieties to be found on the Pacific Northwest coast. Recreational crabbing is a very common summer activity, not to mention a *very* satisfying one. The crabmeat is delicate, sweet, and delicious, and each bite is all the sweeter when personally obtained from a crab pot. Here, the crabmeat is combined with fresh local asparagus and the peppery taste of grated ginger, mixed together with casarecce (cooked al dente, of course).

MAKES 4 SERVINGS

In a large pot of boiling salted water, blanch the asparagus for 2 minutes. Drain and set aside, reserving the water for cooking the pasta.

In a medium-large skillet over medium-low heat, warm the olive oil and butter for 1 to 2 minutes. Add the green onions and sauté for 1 minute. Then add the crabmeat and asparagus and cook for 2 minutes.

Add the wine and continue cooking for another 4 to 5 minutes, until the alcohol has evaporated. Stir in the ginger and season with salt and pepper to taste.

Meanwhile, in the pot previously used for the asparagus, bring the blanching water back to a boil, and cook the casarecce until al dente, drain, and transfer to the skillet. Quickly sauté the pasta and crab-asparagus mixture, adding pasta water as necessary to bind the ingredients.

Plate in four bowls. Finish with some pepper and a drizzle of oil. Enjoy!

Tagliolini con caviale di salmone al profumo di limone e pepe Szechuan /
Tagliolini with Salmon Roe Caviar, Lemon, and Sichuan Pepper

⅓ cup salted artisanal butter
⅓ small shallot, minced
1 sprig thyme, stemmed and finely chopped
Zest of 1 medium organic lemon
Kosher salt and freshly ground white Sichuan pepper
12 ounces tagliolini pasta
10 grams or ⅓ ounce salmon roe caviar
Extra-virgin olive oil

Tip: I am a big fan of red sockeye salmon, and I prefer its roe. Chinook salmon caviar is magnificent, and coho is delicious as well.

Some dishes have one main ingredient that takes center stage, keeping the others in the back like the chorus in an opera performance. In this recipe, Alaskan caviar is the soprano, and the lemon, butter, thyme, and Sichuan pepper are working to make those succulent bright red-orange eggs shine. Salmon roe are unique, with both a briny and sweet taste. Like many luscious ingredients, the best way to prepare them is to touch them as little as possible.

MAKES 4 SERVINGS

In a medium-large skillet over medium-low heat, warm the butter for a minute. Add the shallot, thyme, and half the lemon zest, and sauté for 2 to 3 minutes. Season with salt and Sichuan pepper to taste.

Meanwhile, in a large pot of boiling salted water, cook the tagliolini until al dente. Scoop a bit of the pasta water into the skillet and stir the sauce. Drain the pasta and transfer it to the skillet. Sauté quickly, adding more pasta water as necessary to bind the ingredients.

Plate in four bowls. Finish with the caviar, the remaining lemon zest, a drizzle of oil, and more Sichuan pepper.

Bucatini all'amatriciana con pomodori cimelio di Billy /
Bucatini all'Amatriciana with Billy's Heirloom Tomatoes

4 to 5 medium heirloom tomatoes

1 tablespoon extra-virgin olive oil

5 ounces guanciale cut into ¾-inch strips

½ teaspoon red pepper flakes

¼ cup dry white wine

Kosher salt and freshly ground black pepper

12 ounces bucatini pasta

½ cup grated pecorino

This is a classic all'Amatriciana recipe expressly made to emphasize Billy's heirloom tomatoes. For Seattle food enthusiasts and restaurateurs, Billy's Gardens is an institution when it comes to local prime produce. In the '80s, visionary Billy Allstot and his wife, Stephanie Blackstad, began growing a large selection of vegetables, herbs, plants, and flowers on their Tonasket farm in Okanogan County.

Billy's heirloom tomatoes are the best I have ever had in the region. This is a wonderful example of how nurturing an organic soil can pay off in juiciness and flavor in a *pomodoro* and, consequently, how that perfect tomato can create a spectacular all'Amatriciana when combined with guanciale and perfectly cooked pasta.

MAKES 4 SERVINGS

In a large pot of boiling salted water, blanch the tomatoes for 30 seconds. Remove and quickly run under cold water. Remove the pot from the heat, but do not discard the blanching water. Peel off the tomato skins and remove all the seeds. Crush the tomatoes thoroughly with your clean hands or a fork. Set aside.

In a medium cast-iron skillet over medium-low heat, warm the olive oil for 1 to 2 minutes. Add the guanciale and red pepper flakes, and sauté for 2 minutes. Add the wine and continue cooking until the alcohol has evaporated, 3 to 4 minutes. Remove the guanciale from the pan and set aside, leaving all the oil and liquid it released in the skillet.

Add the tomatoes and cook, stirring occasionally, for 10 to 15 minutes. Season with salt and pepper to taste, keeping in mind that the guanciale and pecorino are rather salty.

In the same pot used to blanch the tomatoes, bring the water back to a boil. Cook the bucatini until al dente, drain, and transfer to the skillet along with the guanciale and half the pecorino. Quickly sauté for a minute, adding pasta water as necessary to bind the ingredients.

Plate in four bowls, top with the remaining ¼ cup pecorino, and serve immediately.

Creste di gallo con melanzane, 'nduja, pomodorini e ricotta salata / **Creste di Gallo with Eggplant, 'Nduja, Supersweet Tomatoes, and Ricotta Salata**

¼ cup extra-virgin olive oil

½ eggplant, cut into ½-inch cubes

1 pound supersweet tomatoes, halved

1 tablespoon 'nduja

Kosher salt and freshly ground black pepper

12 ounces creste di gallo pasta

⅓ cup grated ricotta salata

When the weather turns warmer, I crave juicy, flavorful seasonal vegetables. Both eggplant and tomatoes can be easily found in local farmers' markets and in our gardens in July and August.

Here is a quick recipe that features eggplant and supersweet tomatoes, a variety of small tomatoes similar to cherry tomatoes, but sweeter as the name suggests. The little touch of handmade 'nduja and grated ricotta salata on top makes this simple pasta an exquisite summer dish. ('Nduja is a spreadable fermented *salume* made of pork and Calabrian chili pepper, which gives it a vibrant red color. It originated in Calabria, Italy, and is something that everyone should try at least once.)

MAKES 4 SERVINGS

In a large sauté pan over medium heat, warm the olive oil. When hot (it will bubble if you sprinkle in some flour), fry the eggplant, flipping occasionally, until golden on all sides. Transfer to a tray or large plate covered with paper towel and set aside.

To the sauté pan, add the tomatoes, reduce the heat to medium-low, and cook for 6 to 7 minutes. Using a wooden spoon, gently mix in the 'nduja until it dissolves into the tomatoes. Continue cooking for 6 to 7 minutes, then stir in the eggplant, season with salt and pepper to taste, and turn off the heat.

Meanwhile, in a large pot of boiling salted water, cook the creste di gallo until al dente, drain, and transfer to the sauté pan. Return to medium heat and sauté the pasta and sauce, adding pasta water as necessary to bind the ingredients.

Plate in four bowls. Finish with the ricotta salata, a drizzle of oil, and more pepper.

Pipe con salsiccia all'uva di Chelan e rosmarino / **Pipe with Local Sausage, Chelan Grapes, and Rosemary**

3 tablespoons extra-virgin olive oil

1 small shallot, finely chopped

9 ounces sausage, casing removed

5 ounces grapes

1 sprig rosemary, stemmed

¼ cup vegetable broth

Kosher salt and freshly ground black pepper

¼ cup canola oil

2 large grape leaves, julienned

12 ounces pipe pasta

Pipe con salsiccia all'uva is inspired by a classic Italian recipe with a long history that can be found in *La scienza in cucina e l'arte di mangiar bene*, a famous recipe collection by Pellegrino Artusi published in 1891. This is a recipe firmly for late summer and early fall, when grapes are getting ready to be picked and are crunchy, sweet, and juicy. I am using Chelan grapes here from Succession Wines in Manson, Washington. Both white and red work equally, so choose whichever one you prefer.

MAKES 4 SERVINGS

In a large pan over medium heat, warm the olive oil. Add the shallot and sauté for 1 minute, stirring to avoid burning. Crumble in the sausage, cook for a couple of minutes, add the grapes, and stir. Add the rosemary and cook for 2 minutes more.

Pour in the broth, reduce the heat to low, cover, and cook for 5 minutes. Season with salt and pepper to taste.

In a small pan over high heat, add the canola oil, and fry the grape leaves until crispy. Remove leaves with a spider or slotted spoon, place on a paper towel, and sprinkle with salt.

Meanwhile, in a large pot of boiling salted water, cook the pipe until al dente, drain, and transfer to the large pan. Increase the heat to medium-high, and sauté for a minute, adding pasta water as necessary to bind the ingredients.

Plate in four bowls and finish with the fried grape leaves. Pair with a glass of wine from Succession Wines.

SUMMER

Fall

≋

Casarecce con carbonaro marinato al miso, cavolo cinese e semi di sesamo nero / **Casarecce with Miso-Marinated Alaskan Black Cod, Baby Bok Choy, and Black Sesame Seeds**

¼ cup mirin

¼ cup sake

¼ cup white miso paste

3 tablespoons sugar

10 ounces black cod fillets

5 tablespoons extra-virgin olive oil

1 shallot, finely chopped

2 small baby bok choy, cut into thin strips

Kosher salt and freshly ground black pepper

Red pepper flakes

12 ounces casarecce pasta

1 teaspoon black sesame seeds

Carbonaro—or, as it is commonly known in Italy, *pesce burro* (which literally translates to "butterfish")— belongs to a category of fish unavailable in Europe, causing us to dream about the deep, cold, remote Alaskan ocean waters, an extension of those in Washington State. Living in the PNW, I am always excited for the sablefish season that runs from March to mid-November each year. This recipe is a tribute to Nobu Matsuhisa and his signature dish, black cod in miso, but with the addition of pasta. It's a new take on the classic recipe that still calls for marinating the black cod but skips the oven and uses the stove instead. The result is a quick, irresistible fusion of the Japanese *kasuzuke* tradition (fish or vegetables pickled in sake lees) with Italian pasta. The fish should be marinated for two to three days prior to cooking, so plan accordingly.

MAKES 4 SERVINGS

To prepare the marinade, in a medium saucepan over high heat, bring the mirin and sake to a boil. Wait until the alcohol has evaporated, about a minute, and reduce the heat to low. Slowly stir in the miso paste until it has melted. Increase the heat to high. Add the sugar and energetically whisk until it has dissolved. Transfer the marinade to a mixing bowl and set aside to cool completely.

(→)

Place the black cod in a 10-by-12-inch hotel pan or baking dish, pour the marinade over it, cover with plastic wrap, and refrigerate for 2 to 3 days.

When ready to cook, remove the black cod from the marinade and set aside. In a medium nonstick pan over medium heat, warm the olive oil. Add the shallot and sauté for 1 minute, stirring to avoid burning. Add the baby bok choy, increase the heat medium-high, and stir for a couple of minutes.

Reduce the heat to medium and add the black cod. Cook for 1 minute, allowing the fish to break apart without disintegrating. Add the salt, pepper, and red pepper flakes to taste.

Meanwhile, in a large pot of boiling salted water, cook the casarecce until al dente. Drain, and transfer to the pan; sauté for a minute over medium heat, adding pasta water as necessary to bind the ingredients.

Plate in four bowls. Finish with the black sesame seeds, a drizzle of oil, and more black pepper. Enjoy with sake or a mineral white wine.

Gigli con crema di zucca e cannella, formaggio sirene bulgaro e semi di girasole tostati / **Gigli with Pumpkin Puree, Bulgarian Sirene Cheese, and Toasted Sunflower Seeds**

1 small pumpkin, halved and seeded

2 sprigs rosemary, plus few more for garnish

¼ cup extra-virgin olive oil

¼ cup water

2 ounces pecorino, grated

1 teaspoon cinnamon

Kosher salt and ground white pepper

1 tablespoon unsalted butter

12 ounces gigli pasta

3 ounces Bulgarian sirene cheese

2 tablespoons toasted sunflower seeds

Tip: You can substitute feta cheese for Bulgarian sirene cheese, although Bulgarian cheese is creamier and a little brinier.

Pumpkin equals autumn, and you can customize this lovely seasonal recipe to your own personal taste. Sugar pumpkins work perfectly, but you can use the Italian stripe variety if you prefer something less sweet. I often reach for an international ingredient to make things interesting; here, Bulgarian sirene cheese proves pretty, pungent, and briny. Not to bring up the ubiquitous pumpkin spice latte, but cinnamon also comes to mind when we talk about fall, so I've added it here in the puree. This dish can transform into a soup if the pasta is taken out of the equation.

MAKES 4 SERVINGS

Preheat the oven to 350 degrees F.

Place the pumpkin on a baking sheet. Add the rosemary, olive oil, and water, lightly mix, and cover with aluminum foil. Bake for 40 minutes, or until soft when poked with a fork. Remove the aluminum foil and let the pumpkin cool. Discard the rosemary. Using a spoon, put all the pumpkin pulp in a blender, making sure to add all the juice from the baking sheet. Add the pecorino, cinnamon, and salt and pepper to taste, and blend until creamy.

In a medium pan over medium heat, stir together the pumpkin puree and butter.

Meanwhile, in a large pot of boiling salted water, cook the gigli until al dente, drain, and transfer to the pan. Quickly sauté for a minute, adding pasta water as necessary to bind the ingredients.

Plate in four bowls and crumble the Bulgarian sirene cheese on top. Finish with the sunflower seeds, and garnish with the rosemary sprigs.

≋

Bucatini con crema di cavolfiore e vaniglia, capesante, nocciole arrostite e sommacco / **Bucatini with Cauliflower and Vanilla Bean Puree, Pacific Northwest Baby Pink Scallops, Roasted Hazelnuts, and Sumac**

¼ cup soy sauce

⅓ cup extra-virgin olive oil, divided

1 tablespoon sumac, divided

12 pink scallops

1 small cauliflower, about 1 pound, cut into small pieces

1 Madagascar vanilla bean, sliced lengthwise and seeds scraped

Kosher salt and ground white pepper

¼ cup unsalted butter

¼ cup roasted crushed hazelnuts

12 ounces bucatini pasta

Some ingredients just go together. *Cavolfiori* and *capesante* (cauliflower and scallops) are one of those sexy Italian food combos, often used as antipasto or *secondo piatto di pesce*. The addition of bucatini pasta in this recipe transforms the dish into a delicious *primo piatto*. I am in love with the delicate but complex flavor of PNW pink scallops. The meat is no bigger than a nickel, and their shells are only three inches across, yet their taste is delicate and balanced between sweetness and brightness. Since they are sometimes harder to find, you can substitute the more common but nevertheless delicious sea scallops if necessary.

MAKES 4 SERVINGS

To prepare the marinade, in a small bowl, combine the soy sauce, 3 tablespoons of the olive oil, and ½ tablespoon of the sumac.

Clean and dry the scallops, and put them in a bowl or baking dish. Pour the marinade over them, mix, and refrigerate for a couple of hours.

When ready to cook, preheat the oven to 350 degrees F. On a baking sheet, place the cauliflower and drizzle with 1 tablespoon of the olive oil. Cover with aluminum foil, and bake for 30 minutes, or until soft.

Remove from the oven and let cool, putting aside ½ cup. In a food processor on medium speed, blend the cauliflower and vanilla bean seeds until creamy. Season with salt and pepper to taste.

Remove the scallops from the fridge, drain, and cut eight into small pieces.

In a medium nonstick pan over medium-high heat, warm the butter. Add the remaining four whole scallops and cook for 1 minute on each side. Remove from the pan and set aside.

In the same pan, cook the cut scallops for a minute or so. Add 2 tablespoons of the hazelnuts and sauté for another minute. Stir in the cauliflower puree and remove from the heat.

Meanwhile, in a large pot of boiling salted water, cook the bucatini until al dente, drain, and transfer to the pan. Quickly sauté the pasta with the sauce for a minute, seasoning with salt and pepper and adding pasta water as necessary to bind the ingredients.

Plate in four bowls. Finish each dish with a whole scallop, some of the reserved cauliflower and remaining hazelnuts and sumac, and a drizzle of oil.

Reginette con porcini, speck e zafferano /
Reginette with Pacific Northwest Porcini, Speck, and Saffron

2 tablespoons extra-virgin olive oil

1 shallot, finely chopped

1 clove garlic, gently crushed

6 ounces speck, diced

1 bunch Italian parsley, finely chopped, divided

½ pound fresh porcini mushrooms, cut into ¼-inch slices

¼ teaspoon saffron threads, soaked in 1 tablespoon of boiling water for 15 minutes

Kosher salt and ground white pepper

⅓ cup dry white wine

12 ounces reginette pasta

⅓ cup grated Parmigiano-Reggiano, divided

Tips:

If you have trouble finding speck, you can substitute good-quality bacon.

Trim the earthy base of the porcini with a small paring knife. See page 34 for mushroom-cleaning instructions.

Characterized by a rich, deep forest flavor, *little pigs*—porcini in Italian—are among the most desirable foraged mushrooms. In the PNW, they can be found among pine and fir trees twice a year, during the spring and fall. Porcini mushroom hunters search deep into the wild to find the right soil months before picking them. It's not an easy mushroom to find, but when discovered, it's joy all around! Fresh porcini can be used for a delicious meal right away or can be dried for use throughout the year. For this recipe, we are cooking with fresh porcini.

MAKES 4 SERVINGS

In a large skillet over medium heat, warm the olive oil. Add the shallot and garlic, and cook for a couple of minutes, stirring to avoid burning. Add the speck and cook for another couple of minutes, or until crispy. Add half the parsley and the porcini, and cook for about a minute more. Add the saffron and season with salt and white pepper to taste.

Add the wine and cook for 6 to 7 minutes.

Meanwhile, in a large pot of boiling salted water, cook the reginette until al dente, drain, and transfer to the skillet. Increase the heat to high, and sauté for a minute or so. Stir in half the Parmigiano and pasta water as necessary to bind the ingredients.

Plate in four bowls. Finish with the remaining Parmigiano and parsley, a drizzle of oil and more white pepper.

Conchiglie rigate con crema di zucca delicata, burrata, semi nigella e cayenne africano / **Conchiglie Rigate with Delicata Squash Puree, Burrata, Nigella Seeds, and African Cayenne**

2 medium delicata squashes, halved lengthwise and seeded

¼ cup extra-virgin olive oil

¼ cup water

Kosher salt and freshly ground black pepper

½ cup grated Parmigiano

½ teaspoon nutmeg

12 ounces conchiglie rigate pasta

1 tablespoon butter

2 (8-ounce) burrata

2 tablespoons toasted nigella seeds

1 teaspoon African cayenne

When autumn arrives and you crave pasta but also want a satisfying, comforting soup using the colorful produce from the farmers' market, this is your recipe. It combines the sweetness of the delicata squash and burrata, the heat of the African cayenne, and the crunchiness of the nigella seeds.

MAKES 4 SERVINGS

Preheat the oven to 350 degrees F. On a baking sheet, place the squash, drizzle with the olive oil, add the water, and season with salt and pepper to taste. Bake for 45 minutes, or until fork-tender. Remove from the oven and let cool.

When cool enough to handle, spoon all the squash pulp into a blender, trying to remove as much skin as you can. Add half the Parmigiano and the nutmeg, and blend on low speed until creamy. Transfer to a medium-large skillet.

Meanwhile, in a large pot of boiling salted water, cook the conchiglie rigate until al dente, drain, and transfer to the skillet. Place over medium-high heat, add the butter, and quickly sauté, adding pasta water as necessary to bind the ingredients.

Plate in four bowls. Top with the remaining ¼ cup Parmigiano, half a burrata each, the nigella seeds, and the African cayenne. Serve hot.

Pappardelle con finferli, salsiccia e timo / **Pappardelle with Golden Chanterelles, Sausage, and Thyme**

2 tablespoons extra-virgin olive oil

1 shallot, finely chopped

2 cloves garlic, gently crushed

1 bunch Italian parsley, finely chopped

9 ounces fennel pork sausage, casing removed

2 to 3 thyme sprigs, stemmed

⅓ cup dry white wine

1 pound golden chanterelles, trimmed

Kosher salt and freshly ground black pepper

12 ounces pappardelle pasta

½ cup grated pecorino or Parmigiano

Tip: See page 34 for mushroom-cleaning instructions.

Chanterelles are probably the most foraged mushrooms in the PNW, and keen eyes spot them in the forest under Douglas firs and western hemlocks. Among the several varieties—white, black, and winter or "yellow feet," to mention a few—the golden ones have always been my favorite, not just because of their apricot color, which makes them easier to find, but for their delicate texture. It's a mushroom close to my heart because foraging for *finferli* (Italian for chanterelles) was a common weekend activity for my family when I was growing up in the wet forests of Piedmont.

MAKES 4 SERVINGS

In a large sauté pan over medium heat, warm the olive oil. Add the shallot, garlic, and parsley, and sauté for 2 minutes, or until soft. Add the sausage, using a wooden spoon to break it into pieces. Add the thyme, increase the heat to medium-high, and cook for about 3 minutes. Add the wine and cook it down to let the alcohol evaporate. Add the chanterelles and stir. Season with salt and pepper to taste, reduce the heat to medium, and cook for another 5 to 6 minutes, or until the sausage is cooked through and the mushrooms are crunchy and not mushy.

Meanwhile, in a large pot of boiling salted water, cook the pappardelle until al dente, drain, and transfer to the sauté pan. Increase the heat to high, and sauté for a minute or so, stirring in some pecorino and pasta water as necessary to bind the ingredients.

Plate in four bowls, and finish with some more pecorino, oil, pepper, and thyme. Pair with a glass of young Sangiovese and *buon appetito*!

Tagliolini al tartufo bianco dell'Oregon / **Tagliolini with Oregon White Truffle**

1 Oregon white truffle
   (about 40 grams)
6 tablespoons unsalted
   butter
12 ounces tagliolini
   pasta
Kosher salt
⅓ cup grated
   Parmigiano-Reggiano
Extra-virgin olive oil

Very few culinary experiences can compare to the luscious flavor of Oregon white truffle freshly shaved on top of tagliolini pasta. These precious tubers can be found in Washington State from early fall through spring. *Tartufo—nero* and *bianco—*is a point of national pride in the Piedmont region where I grew up, and is the highlight of the autumn season on the hills of Langhe-Roero and Monferrato.

When cooking with truffles, I apply the same approach as I have with oysters: I touch them as little as possible. To preserve their unique musky and garlicky taste, a little butter and Parmigiano-Reggiano are all that is needed.

MAKES 4 SERVINGS

Clean the truffle with a mushroom brush or a wet cloth to remove the dirt. Using a truffle shaver (or a sharp vegetable peeler), start shaving the truffle. Allow at least 10 grams of truffle per person (or more if you are a truffle lover like me)—half will be placed raw on top of the pasta at the end.

In a medium-large pan over medium heat, melt the butter. Add half the truffle and immediately turn off the heat.

Meanwhile, in a large pot of boiling salted water, cook the pasta until al dente, drain, and transfer to the pan. Over high heat, sauté for a minute or so, stirring in the Parmigiano and pasta water as necessary to bind the ingredients.

Plate in four bowls. Top with the remaining shaved truffle and finish with a drizzle of oil. Pair with a glass or two of Dolcetto d'Alba and celebrate the autumnal season.

Penne con verza saltata, fontina Val D'Aosta, cumino e semi nigella /
Penne with Savoy Cabbage, Fontina, Cumin, and Nigella Seeds

¼ cup extra-virgin olive oil

2 cloves garlic, gently crushed

1 small head savoy cabbage, cut into thin strips

1 tablespoon ground cumin

1 teaspoon red pepper flakes

Kosher salt and freshly ground black pepper

12 ounces penne pasta

4 ounces fontina, shredded

1 tablespoon nigella seeds

This comforting pasta dish is perfect for colder months, when cabbage is ready to be harvested in Oregon, Washington, and British Columbia. The crinkly leaf savoy type is a favorite; great for casseroles and slaw, it's delicious in this satisfying pasta with the melty consistency of the fontina and the aromatic note of the cumin.

MAKES 4 SERVINGS

In a medium-large pan over medium heat, warm the olive oil and garlic.

When the garlic has infused the oil and becomes slightly brown—but not burnt—add the cabbage. Stir in the cumin and red pepper flakes. Reduce the heat to medium-low, cover, and cook for 10 minutes, or until the cabbage is cooked but still crunchy and not completely soft. Season with salt and pepper to taste.

Meanwhile, in a large pot of boiling salted water, cook the penne until al dente, drain, and transfer to the pan. Increase the heat to medium-high, and sauté for 1 minute. Add the fontina and pasta water as necessary to bind the ingredients, and stir energetically until it is incorporated and no big cheese clumps remain.

Plate in four bowls. Finish with a drizzle of oil and a sprinkle of nigella seeds.

≋

Fettuccine con lingcod del Pacific Northwest, cavolfiore viola, olive Castelvetrano e capperi / **Fettuccine with Pacific Northwest Lingcod, Purple Cauliflower, Castelvetrano Olives, and Capers**

6 tablespoons extra-
virgin olive oil

20 Castelvetrano olives,
pitted and halved

1 small shallot, finely
chopped

1 bunch Italian parsley,
minced

1 tablespoon brined
capers, drained

1 teaspoon red pepper
flakes

1 small head purple
cauliflower, cut into
½-inch pieces

10 ounces lingcod fillet,
cut into ½-inch strips

Kosher salt and freshly
ground black pepper

12 ounces fettuccine
pasta

Rockfish is one of the most underrated types of fish on the West Coast. They're delicious. Lingcod belongs to the rockfish family and can be caught from spring through fall, depending on the year. This bottom-dwelling fish has a delightfully mild taste, cooks easily, and is fairly inexpensive.

MAKES 4 SERVINGS

In a medium-large skillet over medium-low heat, warm the olive oil for 1 to 2 minutes. Add the olives, shallot, parsley, capers, and red pepper flakes, and cook for another couple of minutes.

Meanwhile, in a pot of boiling salted water, blanch the cauliflower for 2 minutes. Save the water for cooking the pasta.

Strain out the cauliflower and transfer it to the skillet. Increase the heat to medium and cook for 2 minutes. Reduce the heat to medium-low, add the lingcod, and cook for another 5 to 6 minutes. Season with salt and pepper to taste.

Return the pot with the blanching water to a boil, then cook the fettuccine until al dente, drain, and transfer to the skillet. Increase the heat to high, and quickly sauté, adding pasta water as necessary to bind the ingredients.

Plate in four bowls. Finish with a drizzle of oil and more black pepper, and enjoy!

Orecchiette con cozze Penn Cove, ceci e capperi / **Orecchiette with Penn Cove Mussels, Chickpeas, and Capers**

¼ cup extra-virgin olive oil

½ shallot, minced

4 cloves garlic, gently crushed

1 bunch Italian parsley, stemmed and leaves minced

1 tablespoon brined capers, drained

Freshly ground black pepper

1 small fresh peperoncino, minced, or ¼ teaspoon red pepper flakes

10 cherry tomatoes, halved (optional)

3 pounds Penn Cove mussels

¼ cup dry white wine

½ cup cooked chickpeas, drained

Kosher salt and freshly ground black pepper

12 ounces orecchiette pasta

Pitted Gaeta olives, for garnish

Available year-round, Penn Cove mussels are one of Washington's most iconic shellfish and are shipped all over the country. These succulent bivalves are harvested about sixty miles northwest of Seattle in the waters off Whidbey Island; there, you'll find the oldest commercial mussel farm in North America. Meaty and sweet at the same time, Penn Cove mussels go great with simple ingredients that don't overpower them. This pasta dish is inspired by the southern Italian tradition of *cozze* (mussels) and legumes.

MAKES 4 SERVINGS

In a large deep skillet over medium heat, warm the olive oil for a minute. Add the shallot, garlic, half the parsley, the capers, pepper to taste, and the peperoncino, and cook for about 2 minutes. Add the tomatoes and the mussels, stir, and cook for 1 minute.

Add the wine and continue cooking until the alcohol evaporates, 2 to 3 minutes. Reduce the heat to low, add the chickpeas, cover, and let cook for 5 minutes.

Meanwhile, in a large pot of boiling salted water, cook the orecchiette until al dente, drain, and transfer to the skillet. Increase the heat to medium-high, and sauté for a minute, adding pasta water as necessary to bind the ingredients.

Plate in four bowls. Finish with the remaining parsley, a few Gaeta olives, and a drizzle of oil.

How to clean mussels

In a colander in the kitchen sink, run the mussels under cold water. Rinse them repeatedly, until the water runs clear, making sure all the dirt is gone. Next, remove the beard from each mussel: Pull on the clump of fibers with focused energy, taking care not to break the shell. Use a towel if they seem too slippery to hold. Rinse again, then proceed with cooking.

Orecchiette con scarola, 'nduja e burrata / **Orecchiette with Escarole, 'Nduja, and Burrata**

3 tablespoons extra-virgin olive oil

2 cloves garlic, gently crushed

1 medium head escarole, finely chopped

2 ounces artisanal 'nduja, divided

Kosher salt and freshly ground black pepper

12 ounces orecchiette pasta

½ cup grated Parmigiano-Reggiano, divided

9 ounces burrata

Fall is the best time for escarole, and the PNW offers an ideal climate for planting and harvesting these greens, which are crunchy and slightly bitter when raw but sweeter when cooked. In this recipe, I am using a local 'nduja made by my friend Stano Riccio, but you can often find it at Italian specialty stores. 'Nduja is a soft, spreadable spicy pork *salume* originally from Calabria. Good 'nduja should have zero preservatives because of the chili, which acts as a natural preservative. In addition, authentic 'nduja shouldn't contain garlic or other spices.

MAKES 4 SERVINGS

In a medium-large sauté pan over medium heat, warm the olive oil and garlic for a couple of minutes, stirring to avoid burning.

Add the escarole, cover, and cook for 8 to 10 minutes, or until the escarole has wilted. Add half the 'nduja and stir until it melts into the escarole mixture. Season with salt and pepper to taste. Turn off the heat, but leave the pan on the burner.

Meanwhile, in a large pot of boiling salted water, cook the orecchiette until al dente, drain, and transfer to the sauté pan. Over medium-high heat, sauté the pasta for a minute, adding half the Parmigiano and pasta water as necessary to bind the ingredients.

Plate in four bowls. Finish with the remaining ¼ cup Parmigiano, the remaining 1 ounce 'nduja, scoops of the burrata, and a drizzle of oil. Enjoy!

Rigatoni con crema di romanesco, pecorino e bacon croccante /
Rigatoni with Romanesco Puree, Pecorino, and Crunchy Bacon

4 strips bacon

1 medium head romanesco, cut into small pieces

¾ cup grated pecorino

3 tablespoons extra-virgin olive oil, divided

2 cloves garlic

1 to 2 pinches red pepper flakes, or 1 small peperoncino, minced

Kosher salt and freshly ground black pepper

12 ounces rigatoni pasta

Tip: Bacon can be swapped out for pancetta, speck, or guanciale. Romanesco can be substituted with broccoli.

This is an easy, approachable dish that belongs firmly in fall, when romanesco is at its best. Rich in vitamins C and K, romanesco is not just delicious but also gorgeous with its distinctive texture and bright-green color. I added bacon to this recipe for two reasons: first, it provides a crispy, crunchy topping, and second, it's a fridge staple that many of us have on hand.

MAKES 4 SERVINGS

Preheat the oven to 400 degrees F. On a baking sheet (lined with parchment paper, if you like), place the bacon, and bake for 15 to 18 minutes, or until crispy. Set aside until cool, then cut into ½-inch pieces.

In a large pot of boiling salted water, put half the romanesco. Cook until soft, 5 to 6 minutes. Using a spider, remove the romanesco and set aside. Turn off the heat, but keep the pot of water to use later for cooking the pasta.

In a blender, blend the cooked romanesco, half the pecorino, and 1 tablespoon of the olive oil until creamy and smooth.

In a medium-large pan over medium heat, warm the remaining 2 tablespoons olive oil, the garlic, and red pepper flakes for a minute. Stir in the romanesco puree, and continue cooking for another couple of minutes. Season with salt and pepper to taste. Turn off the heat, but leave the pan on the burner.

Meanwhile, bring the pot of water back to a boil, add the remaining romanesco and the rigatoni and cook until al dente. Drain and transfer to the pan. Quickly sauté, adding pasta water as necessary to bind the ingredients.

Plate in four bowls, and finish with the remaining pecorino, the bacon pieces, and a drizzle of oil. Enjoy!

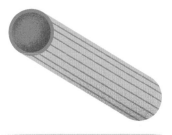

Winter

Spaghetti alla Chitarra ai ricci di mare del Pacific Northwest e mollica di pane tostata al limone / **Spaghetti alla Chitarra with Pacific Northwest Sea Urchin and Toasted Lemon Bread Crumbs**

2 slices rustic bread

4 tablespoons extra-virgin olive oil, divided

1 medium organic lemon

1 bunch Italian parsley, finely chopped

1 Calabrian chili pepper

2 cloves garlic

4 ounces sea urchin roe

12 ounces spaghetti alla Chitarra pasta

Kosher salt and freshly ground black pepper

If I had to pick a last meal, this would probably be it. *Spaghetti ai ricci di mare* evokes the clean ocean scent: sweet and crisp at the same time. Sea urchin is the quintessential sensual fruit of the sea—the parts that we eat are the gonads of both male and female urchins! They offer up a flavor reminiscent of my childhood, when dive masters and a few adventurous family friends would dive to the bottom of the Mediterranean Sea and return with these gifts from Mother Nature, ready to be opened and cooked with spaghetti. In the Pacific Northwest, sea urchins are caught by commercial dive masters in December and January when the cold temperatures of the water allow the urchins to spawn. These gorgeous Pacific purple sea urchins with pasta is something everyone should try at least once in their lives.

MAKES 4 SERVINGS

Preheat the oven to 350 degrees F. On a baking sheet, place the bread, and drizzle 1 tablespoon of the olive oil over it. Bake for about 20 minutes. Remove the bread from the oven and let cool to room temperature. Put the bread slices in a blender. Using a microplane, zest the lemon into the blender. Pulse until you obtain a fine consistency, then set aside.

In a medium skillet over medium-low heat, warm the remaining 3 tablespoons olive oil. Add three-quarters of the parsley, the chili pepper, and garlic, and cook for about 2 minutes, stirring to avoid burning. Increase the heat to medium and add half the roe, stirring for 1 minute. Turn off the heat, but leave the pan on the burner.

Meanwhile, in a large pot of boiling salted water, cook the spaghetti until al dente, drain, and transfer to the skillet, adding some of the pasta water as necessary to bind the ingredients. Add the remaining parsley and sauté for a minute. Season with salt and pepper to taste.

Plate in four bowls. Finish with the bread crumbs, the remaining roe, and a drizzle of oil. Eat while hot.

How to cut open a sea urchin

Place a whole sea urchin upside down, making sure to have access to the mouth. Hold the urchin with a towel, and using kitchen shears, cut a hole close to the perimeter of the skeleton. Remove that part of the shell and look at the beautiful star-shaped flower that has been revealed to you. Scoop out the roe and use it for pasta, risotto, or crostini.

Fusilli con pesto di salvia e pinoli, uova di quaglia e pepe di Aleppo / Fusilli with Pine Nut and Sage Pesto, Quail Eggs, and Aleppo Pepper

1 clove garlic

1 ounce pine nuts

35 medium sage leaves

½ cup extra-virgin olive oil

½ cup grated Parmigiano-Reggiano

Kosher salt and freshly ground black pepper

¼ cup canola oil

12 ounces fusilli pasta

4 quail eggs

1 tablespoon Aleppo pepper

Tips:

You can use a food processor or blender if you don't have a mortar and pestle. Just make sure to use the pulse setting.

Pecorino can be substituted for Parmigiano-Reggiano, walnuts for pine nuts, and you can cook the eggs over easy or lightly boil them if you want to avoid raw eggs.

Sage is all the rage in the Pacific Northwest: clary sage, silver sage, cooking sage, the variations go on. It grows profusely with almost zero care and embellishes many front yards all year long. High in antioxidants, this aromatic herb can be of great use in a pesto. Here's a recipe for those who like pungent flavors, sweetened by a raw quail egg and spiced up by Aleppo pepper.

MAKES 4 SERVINGS

Using a mortar and pestle, grind the garlic and pine nuts into a paste. Add 30 of the sage leaves and continue to grind against the walls of the mortar until the sage leaves are reduced to small pieces. Slowly drizzle in the olive oil, continuing to grind, and add the Parmigiano. Season with salt and pepper to taste, and grind until the pesto is creamy. Set aside.

In a small pan over high heat, warm the canola oil. When the oil is hot, fry the remaining 5 sage leaves for about 1 minute. Once fried, remove with a slotted spoon, place on a paper towel, and set aside.

Meanwhile, in a large pot of boiling salted water, cook the fusilli until al dente, drain, and transfer to a mixing bowl. Add the pesto and quickly combine.

Plate in four bowls, and crack one quail egg on top of each bowl, keeping the yolk intact. Sprinkle with the Aleppo pepper, and finish with the sage leaves and a drizzle of oil.

Orecchiette con salsiccia calabrese piccante sbriciolata e cime di rapa /
Orecchiette with Crumbled Calabrian Spicy Sausage and Rapini

2 pounds rapini, divided into florets

3 tablespoons extra-virgin olive oil

2 cloves garlic, gently crushed

4 spicy Calabrian chili sausages, casings removed

⅓ cup dry white wine

Kosher salt and freshly ground black pepper

1 fresh Italian peperoncino, cut into small pieces

12 ounces orecchiette pasta

⅓ cup pecorino

This is a quintessential dish of Apulia, a region in southern Italy. There are two reasons why I've included it here. The first is that rapini grows magnificently in the PNW—it loves the mild climate. The second is that there are several local sustainable meat producers that make delicious spicy Italian sausage (see page 153). The result is an ideal example of how to make a traditional Italian recipe using local ingredients.

MAKES 4 SERVINGS

In a medium-large pot of boiling salted water, blanch the rapini for 3 minutes. Using a spider or slotted spoon, remove them and set aside. Keep the water for cooking the pasta later.

In a medium pan over medium heat, warm the olive oil and garlic. Once the garlic has infused the oil but before it burns, add the sausage, breaking it up as much as possible. Cook for a couple of minutes, add the wine, and continue cooking until the alcohol evaporates. Season with salt and pepper to taste, add the peperoncino and rapini, and sauté for about 2 minutes.

Bring the blanching water back to a boil, cook the orecchiette until al dente, drain, and transfer to the pan. Increase the heat to medium-high, and sauté for a minute, adding pasta water as necessary to bind the ingredients. Stir in the pecorino.

Plate in four bowls. Finish with more pecorino and a drizzle of oil. Enjoy with a great medium-bodied red wine.

≋

Casarecce con vongole Manila clams, ceci e pomodorini / **Casarecce with Pacific Northwest Manila Clams, Chickpeas, and Cherry Tomatoes**

2½ pounds Manila clams

2 tablespoons extra-virgin olive oil

1 small shallot, chopped

1 small bunch Italian parsley, finely chopped

2 cloves garlic, gently crushed

1 tablespoon brined capers, drained

Freshly ground black pepper

Red pepper flakes

1 cup cooked chickpeas, drained

10 cherry tomatoes, halved

⅓ cup dry white wine

12 ounces casarecce pasta

———————

Tip: If you don't have time to cook dried chickpeas, you can use good-quality canned ones (rinsed and drained first, of course).

I love Manila clams, especially in the winter months, because like many other bivalves, they are best harvested and enjoyed during colder weather. The Pacific Northwest is also home to savory and varnish clams, great alternatives to Manilas. They are less meaty but juicy and have a gorgeous purple shell. Clam digging on the Olympic Peninsula was one of the first outdoor activities I did when I moved to Seattle.

MAKES 4 SERVINGS

To clean the clams, soak them in plenty of cold water, rinsing several times and checking that the sand is completely removed.

In a large sauté pan over medium heat, warm the olive oil. Add the shallot, parsley, garlic, capers, and black pepper and red pepper flakes to taste, and sauté for 2 to 3 minutes. Then add the chickpeas.

Drain the clams, add them to the pan, and sauté for about 2 minutes. Add the tomatoes and wine, and cook for about 3 minutes, or until the alcohol has evaporated. Cover and cook until the clams have opened, 4 to 5 minutes.

Meanwhile, in a large pot of boiling salted water, cook the casarecce until al dente, drain, and transfer to the pan. Increase the heat to high, and sauté for 1 minute, adding pasta water as necessary to bind the ingredients.

Plate in four bowls. Finish with some parsley, a drizzle of oil, and more black pepper to taste.

WINTER

117

Spaghettoni con purea di rape rosse, burrata, basilico e olio di peperoncino calabrese / **Spaghettoni with Red Beet Pesto, Burrata, Basil, and Calabrian Chili Oil**

2 large red beets, well scrubbed

1 cup water

1 cup extra-virgin olive oil, divided

Kosher salt and freshly ground black pepper

1½ cups grated pecorino romano, divided

1 small Yukon Gold potato, boiled and cooled

12 ounces spaghettoni pasta

2 (2-ounce) balls burrata

¼ cup Calabrian chili oil

8 fresh basil leaves

Freshly cracked black pepper

Beets are not the most common vegetable in Italy, but my mother always loved them, and consequently, I have fond childhood memories of their distinctive earthy smell when baked. In particular, she used to make a sort of caprese salad with them, pairing a slice of red beet with a slice of mozzarella, which took on a beautiful pink tone. As a kid, I was fascinated by this and ate it more for the color than the flavor. Seattle is much more beet-forward, and it has been a joy to cook with them, especially golden beets. This dish is a stunner for the eyes and the taste buds.

MAKES 4 SERVINGS

Preheat the oven to 350 degrees F. In a baking pan, place the beets, water, ⅓ cup of the olive oil, and salt and pepper to taste. Cover with foil and bake for about 1 hour, or until the beets can be easily pierced by a fork.

Remove the beets from the oven, uncover, and allow to cool. In a large bowl, add the beets and their cooking liquid, 1 cup of the pecorino, the potato, and salt and pepper to taste. Using an immersion blender or a mixer on low speed, blend until creamy but not liquid. Pour the puree into a large skillet and set aside.

Meanwhile, in a large pot of boiling salted water, cook the spaghettoni until al dente, drain, and transfer to the skillet. Over high heat, sauté the pasta and beet puree for a minute, adding pasta water as necessary to bind the ingredients. Sprinkle the remaining ½ cup pecorino into the skillet, stir, and remove from heat.

Plate in four bowls, using a large serving fork to twist the pasta so that it resembles a nest. Top with a spoonful of burrata, a drizzle of Calabrian chili oil, and a couple of fresh basil leaves. Finish with cracked black pepper.

Radiatori con crema di carote invernali, mozzarella di bufala, semi nigella e curcuma / Radiatori with Pacific Northwest Winter Carrot Puree, Buffalo Mozzarella, Nigella Seeds, and Turmeric

2 tablespoons extra-virgin olive oil

1 small shallot, finely chopped

4 to 5 medium carrots (8 to 10 ounces), cut into ½-inch rounds

½ cup water

1 teaspoon turmeric

½ cup grated Parmigiano

¼ cup fresh cow ricotta

Kosher salt and freshly ground black pepper

12 ounces radiatori pasta

2 (2-ounce) balls buffalo mozzarella

1 tablespoon nigella seeds

This recipe from my childhood carries the sweetness and color of cooked carrots. It's accentuated by the *curcuma* (turmeric), resulting in an explosion of flavor.

Like many root crops, carrots grow very well in all regions of Washington and Oregon. Although they are a year-round veggie, I love to consider them a winter one, especially when cooked. Buffalo mozzarella, with its slightly sour taste, is the cherry on top—literally—of this recipe.

MAKES 4 SERVINGS

In a medium-large skillet over medium heat, warm the olive oil. Add the shallot and sauté for a couple of minutes, then stir in the carrots. Add the water and turmeric, stir again, and cover. Reduce the heat to medium-low and cook for 10 to 15 minutes, or until the carrots are soft.

Uncover and transfer to a blender with the Parmigiano, ricotta, and salt and pepper to taste. Blend until creamy. Return the carrot puree to the skillet.

Meanwhile, in a large pot of boiling salted water, cook the radiatori until al dente, drain, and transfer to the skillet. Increase the heat to high, and sauté for a minute, adding pasta water as necessary to bind the ingredients.

Plate in four bowls and top each with a spoonful of buffalo mozzarella in the center. Finish with an additional sprinkle of turmeric, the nigella seeds, and a drizzle of oil.

Tagliolini al nero di seppia, cannellini e bottarga di muggine / **Squid Ink Tagliolini with Cannellini Beans and Bottarga**

2 tablespoons extra-virgin olive oil
1 bunch Italian parsley, finely minced
3 cloves garlic, gently crushed
1 tablespoon brined capers, drained
Pinch of red pepper flakes
4 to 5 (0.14-ounce) sachets squid ink
1 pound squid, cut into small pieces
⅓ cup dry white wine
⅓ cup cooked cannellini beans, drained
8 cherry tomatoes, halved
Kosher salt and freshly ground black pepper
12 ounces tagliolini pasta
1 bottarga (about 5 ounces)

Tip: Since tomatoes are not in season during PNW winters, they are an optional (but tasty) addition.

This gorgeous dish beautifully marries the tangy ocean flavor of squid ink and the rich, briny taste of bottarga (fish-cured roe).

Squidding is a fun winter activity best done at night on your local pier with the help of a rod outfitted with a specific squid jig and a good LED light panel. Extracting the ink out of a squid is not difficult, although it requires some technique (see page 124). It's very satisfying to see the dramatic black ink coming out of the glands and sacs of the squid, and the taste is unique. Bottarga is an ancient Italian specialty that carries with it the taste of Mediterranean caviar. It can be found in other countries such as Portugal, Tunisia, Turkey, and Japan, and is usually made of mullet or tuna roe.

MAKES 4 SERVINGS

In a large pan over medium-high heat, warm the olive oil. Add the parsley, garlic, capers, and red pepper flakes and sauté for 2 minutes. Stir in the squid ink.

Add the squid meat, cook for a minute, stir, and add the wine. Reduce the heat to medium-low and cook for 5 to 7 minutes, or until the alcohol evaporates.

Add the cannellini beans and tomatoes, season with salt and pepper to taste, stir, and turn off the heat.

Meanwhile, in a large pot of boiling salted water, cook the tagliolini until al dente, drain, and transfer to the skillet. Over high heat, sauté the pasta for a minute, adding pasta water as necessary to bind the ingredients.

Carefully plate (squid ink will stain) in four bowls, and wipe each with a wet paper towel around the edges for a clean presentation.

Using a microplane, shave a couple of paper-thin pieces of the bottarga on top of each dish. Finish with fresh parsley, a drizzle of oil, and more black pepper. Enjoy immediately.

How to clean and extract ink from a squid

You can catch a squid yourself, or purchase a fresh whole one at your local fish market. Either way, start by washing it thoroughly under cold water.

To extract the ink, separate the head from the tentacles, pulling the head away. The ink sac should be visible; it resembles a black vein. Remove it with your finger or a small knife, then pierce the sac and collect the ink in a small cup. Squid have another sac behind their eyes: use the same removal technique, then pierce and extract the ink there as well. When using squid ink in pasta or risotto, keep in mind that it is delicious yet intense, so adjust the quantity accordingly.

To clean the squid meat, first remove the skin by simply peeling it off. Wash the tube under cold water, removing the innards with your fingers. Chop to your preferred thickness. I like to cut the tube into rings with kitchen shears. Both the body and tentacles are edible.

Bucatini con puttanesca al geoduck del Pacific Northwest / **Bucatini with Pacific Northwest Geoduck Puttanesca**

4 to 5 tablespoons extra-virgin olive oil

5 to 7 drained anchovy fillets

1 bunch Italian parsley, finely minced

3 cloves garlic, gently crushed

½ pound geoduck, cut into thin slices

⅓ cup Gaeta olives, pitted

2 tablespoons brined capers, drained

1 teaspoon red pepper flakes

14 ounces (1¾ cups) canned San Marzano tomato puree

Kosher salt and freshly ground black pepper

12 ounces bucatini pasta

A magnificent clam lives in the waters of the PNW, from Puget Sound to British Columbia and all the way north to Alaska. I'm talking about the geoduck. Both sweet and briny, this impressive creature can be harvested in the winter months during low tide at certain beaches and state parks.

I still remember the first time I tagged along with my friend Nathan and his crew on the Olympic Peninsula and helped the diggers wading in cold, muddy waters to harvest geoducks. It was not easy extracting them, because you need enough strength to pull them at least two feet to the surface, but it was definitely rewarding to bring them back to the kitchen to create some delicious dishes. Here, I offer my reinterpretation of classic puttanesca . . . with a PNW twist.

MAKES 4 SERVINGS

In a medium-large sauté pan over medium heat, warm the olive oil. Add the anchovy fillets, parsley, and garlic, and sauté for about 2 minutes, or until the anchovies can break into pieces.

Add the geoduck and cook for a minute. Add the olives, capers, and red pepper flakes, and cook for another minute. Reduce the heat to medium-low, add the tomato puree, and cook for about 10 minutes. Season with salt and pepper to taste.

Meanwhile, in a large pot of boiling salted water, cook the bucatini until al dente, drain, and transfer to the sauté pan. Increase the heat to high and sauté the pasta for a minute, adding pasta water as necessary to bind the ingredients.

Plate in four bowls and finish with some fresh parsley.

How to clean and cut a geoduck

Clean the geoduck under cold running water, making sure all the dirt and sand are gone. Set aside. Boil a large pot of water, remove from heat, and submerge the geoduck for 30 seconds. Using tongs, transfer it to a cutting board.

The shell should be able to slip off; remove it along with the gut. Now you are left with two parts of the geoduck: the siphon (neck) and the mantle (breast). Remove the thick skin with your hands or a small knife.

Cut the breast from the neck and set aside. The breast—body meat—has a stronger clam flavor and can be cut into small pieces and used in recipes like chowder. The neck has a wonderful crunchy texture and can be used in various ways, from sashimi to puttanesca.

Ziti con patate, pancetta e scamorza affumicata / **Ziti with Potatoes, Pancetta, and Smoked Scamorza**

2 tablespoons extra-virgin olive oil

3 to 4 ounces pancetta

2 medium Yukon Gold potatoes, cut into ½-inch cubes

2 sprigs rosemary

12 ounces ziti pasta

Kosher salt and freshly ground black pepper

4 ounces smoked scamorza or provola, shredded

½ cup grated Parmigiano-Reggiano or Grana Padano

Tips:

Bacon can be used instead of pancetta.

This recipe usually requires about 2 cups of water, but the exact amount can vary since each pasta cooks differently.

Use the cooking time on the pasta package as a guideline for how long it will take.

This classic pasta dish is a tribute to Naples. It is traditionally served with *pasta mista* (a mixture of different types of short pasta). Beyond the terrific combination of ingredients, its preparation is unusual because the pasta is cooked along with the rest of the dish and not separately in a pot of boiling salted water. It's basically a *pasta risottata*, a pasta cooked like a risotto.

For me, what makes this a specifically PNW pasta is using the amazing scamorza *affumicata* from Twin Sisters Creamery in Whatcom County, in northwestern Washington near the Canadian border. This recipe calls for any smoked provola or scamorza, so feel free to pick up one from your favorite local creamery.

MAKES 4 SERVINGS

In a medium-large skillet over medium-high heat, warm the olive oil. Add the pancetta and sauté for a couple of minutes, or until crispy.

Add the potatoes and rosemary and cook for 2 minutes. Stir in 1 cup of water. Reduce the heat to medium-low and add the pasta. Stir constantly, as if you are making risotto, adding more water, a little bit at a time as needed, until both the pasta and potatoes are cooked through. It should be a loose consistency, not too soupy or too thick. Season with salt and pepper to taste. Remove the rosemary sprigs from the skillet.

Turn off the heat, energetically stir in the smoked scamorza and Parmigiano. Serve hot and finish with more pepper.

Rigatoni con ragù di alce / **Rigatoni with Pacific Northwest Elk Ragù, Juniper Berries, and Bay Leaves**

3 tablespoons extra-virgin olive oil

⅓ cup diced white onion

⅓ cup diced carrots

⅓ cup diced celery

1 pound ground elk

½ cup red wine

16 ounces (2 cups) canned San Marzano tomato puree

1 cup water

10 juniper berries

10 black peppercorns

4 to 5 bay leaves

2 whole cloves

12 ounces rigatoni pasta

¼ cup unsalted butter

¾ cup grated Parmigiano-Reggiano, divided

Tip: Elk can be substituted with venison or deer meat.

A slow-cooked ragù recipe is perfect during cold and rainy months, and elk is among my favorite game meat for its clean, sweet taste. The Northwest has an abundance of elk, and hunting them is a common activity across Washington State, from Yakima to Mount St. Helens and the Olympic Peninsula. Juniper berries, bay leaves, and cloves blend with all the other flavors to make this pasta a truly special dish to serve.

MAKES 4 SERVINGS

In a deep medium skillet over medium heat, warm the olive oil. Add the onion, carrots, and celery (the trio is called *soffritto* in Italian cooking), and sauté for 2 to 3 minutes. Add the elk and cook, stirring occasionally, for 3 to 4 minutes. Add the wine and continue cooking for another 2 to 3 minutes, until the alcohol evaporates. Stir in the tomato puree and water.

Add the juniper berries, black peppercorns, bay leaves, and cloves, reduce the heat to low, and simmer for about 3 hours, stirring occasionally. If the ragù is getting too thick, add a little bit of extra water.

Meanwhile, in a large pot of boiling salted water, cook the rigatoni until al dente and drain. In a mixing bowl, quickly stir together the rigatoni, half the ragù, and the butter, until the butter has melted, adding pasta water as necessary to bind the ingredients.

Stir in half the Parmigiano, and divide among four bowls. Finish each bowl with a scoop of the remaining ragù and the remaining Parmigiano. Enjoy with a full-bodied red wine.

Pasta e fagioli / **Pasta and Beans**

10 ounces dry navy
   beans
2 to 3 bay leaves
2 tablespoons extra-
   virgin olive oil
2 cloves garlic, gently
   crushed
1 bunch Italian parsley,
   minced
1 teaspoon red pepper
   flakes
1 tablespoon tomato
   paste
1 (14-ounce) can whole
   peeled San Marzano
   tomatoes, drained
Kosher salt and freshly
   ground black pepper
12 ounces pasta mista
   or ditalini pasta
⅓ cup grated
   Parmigiano-Reggiano

Tips:

If you happen to
have a Parmigiano-
Reggiano rind, this is
a perfect way to use
it: simply put it in the
pot with the pasta.

Pasta e fagioli is a
classic and makes for
delicious leftovers.

Pasta e fagioli is one of the most popular national
Italian dishes, with countless versions from north to
south. Here is a special Pacific Northwest version.
Beans grow well in the region, in particular pinto
beans, black beans, navy beans, and kidney beans.
Here, I've used navy beans, also called pea beans. Not
to be confused with cannellini, this variety of small
white bean cooks faster and has a velvety, nutty taste,
making it a comforting pasta dish for long rainy
winter days.

Traditionally, *pasta e fagioli* is made with *pasta
mista*, a mix of several pasta shapes. Ditalini works
well too.

MAKES 4 SERVINGS

In a pot full of cold water, soak the beans for at least 7 to
8 hours. (These can soak the night before.)

When thoroughly soaked, rinse and drain the beans. Fill the
pot with fresh cold water and add the bay leaves. Place
over medium heat, and cook for about 20 minutes.

Meanwhile, in another pot over medium-low heat, warm
the olive oil. Add the garlic, parsley, and red pepper flakes,
and sauté for 1 to 2 minutes, stirring to avoid burning. Stir
in the tomato paste and tomatoes, and cook for 10 to
15 minutes.

(→)

When the beans are cooked, but still firm and al dente, remove them with a spider or slotted spoon and transfer to the other pot with the tomatoes. Season with salt and pepper to taste.

At this point the consistency will be pretty thick, but if it's excessively thick, add some water. Add the pasta to the pot and cook until al dente. (This is an unconventional way to cook pasta, but a classic one when we talk about *pasta e fagioli*. The pasta will release gluten in the pot and the result will be incredibly creamy.)

Plate in four bowls. Finish with the Parmigiano, a drizzle of oil, and more black pepper.

Pappardelle con ragù bianco di coniglio, melograno e pepe rosa / **Pappardelle with Tomato-less Rabbit Ragù, Pomegranate, and Pink Pepper**

3 tablespoons extra-virgin olive oil

½ white onion, finely chopped

1 carrot, finely chopped

1 stick celery, finely chopped

1 pound ground local rabbit

3 ounces pancetta, cut into ½-inch cubes

2 sprigs rosemary

10 to 15 pink peppercorns

Kosher salt

¼ cup dry white wine

1 cup organic chicken stock

Seeds from 1 pomegranate, divided

12 ounces pappardelle pasta

½ cup grated Parmigiano-Reggiano, divided

I grew up with *coniglio al forno*—roasted rabbit—for our Sunday lunch. It was a delicious, juicy, and crunchy *secondo piatto* that my mom still prepares for me when I go back home. This version is a colorful holiday pasta dish inspired by my childhood, pairing the tenderness of the rabbit with tart pomegranate, a holiday symbol of prosperity and good luck.

We have wonderful organic rabbit farms in Washington, and Valley Rabbits is one of them. Sourcing from small sustainable farms means you're purchasing great meat *and* getting to know the territory better.

MAKES 4 SERVINGS

In a medium deep saucepan over medium heat, warm the olive oil for a minute. Add the onion, carrots, and celery, and sauté for 2 minutes.

Add the rabbit and pancetta, and cook for 4 to 5 minutes, stirring constantly. Add the rosemary and pink peppercorns. Season with salt to taste. Stir and continue cooking for another 2 to 3 minutes.

Add a splash of the wine and let it evaporate. Add the stock, cover, reduce the heat to low, and simmer for about 2 hours. When the meat is cooked through and the sauce comes together, uncover and add half the pomegranate seeds (also called *arils*).

Meanwhile, in a large pot of boiling salted water, cook the pappardelle until al dente, drain, and transfer to the saucepan. Quickly sauté, adding pasta water as necessary to bind the ingredients.

Stir in half the Parmigiano, and divide among four bowls. Finish with the remaining ¼ cup Parmigiano, the remaining pomegranate seeds, and a drizzle of oil. Enjoy with a glass or two of smooth and young red wine.

Anytime

Pasta al Pomodoro / **Pasta with Traditional San Marzano Tomato Sauce**

¼ cup extra-virgin olive oil

½ shallot, finely chopped

2 cloves garlic, gently crushed

1 (28-ounces) can whole peeled San Marzano tomatoes, drained

½ cup water

1 fresh basil sprig, stemmed

½ teaspoon dried oregano

Kosher salt and freshly ground black pepper

12 ounces of your favorite fresh or dried pasta

½ cup grated Parmigiano-Reggiano

Without any doubt, this is *the* quintessential pasta dish Italians love to eat and cook, north or south, all year round. *Pomo-d'oro* means "golden apple" in Italian, and tomato sauce is among the first recipes a child or teenager learns how to cook in an Italian kitchen. It was definitely my first. That said, there are countless recipes for a pomodoro sauce, all similar but not the same. San Marzano tomatoes are the ideal variety for the dish, but others can do the job as well. You can make a delicious *sugo di pomodoro* with fresh tomatoes, but since we want to make this recipe year-round, it calls for *pelati*, canned peeled tomatoes religiously made at the end of the summer and stored in the kitchen for the whole year.

Cooking times for the sauce can vary. If you want something lighter that leans into the fruity juiciness of the tomatoes, cook it for a shorter time. If you are seeking something heartier and denser, cook it for longer. But there is one thing everyone can agree on: adding sugar to tomato sauce is a sacrilege; it's an old trick to correct the acidity of overripe tomatoes.

If you are using canned peeled tomatoes, look at the ingredients list and select a can that uses the fewest ingredients. High-fructose corn syrup, calcium chloride, garlic, and oregano should be avoided, while salt, basil, and citric acid (an acidity regulator) are acceptable.

MAKES 4 SERVINGS

The absolute best way of cooking *sugo di pomodoro* is in a terra-cotta pot, if you have one. The heat uniformly spreads from the bottom to the top and across the sides of the pot. Italians believe that it gives a unique, delicious taste to the sauce.

Instead of crushing the tomatoes by hand, you could use a blender, but take care to not liquefy the tomatoes.

Pasta al Pomodoro is one of the few dishes where it's acceptable to use any pasta shape you like: long, short, wide, ridged, or smooth. Try a few different shapes to see which you prefer.

In a medium pot over medium heat, warm the olive oil. Add the shallot and garlic, and sauté for 2 minutes, stirring to avoid burning.

Put the tomatoes in a medium mixing bowl and crush them with your hands. Add the crushed tomatoes to the pot. In the same mixing bowl, add the water and swirl. Add this tomato water to the pot and stir.

To the pot, add the basil, oregano, and salt and pepper to taste. Let the leaves wilt, then reduce the heat to low. Let the sugo simmer for 30 to 40 minutes, depending on the desired thickness.

In a large pot of boiling salted water, cook the pasta until al dente (following the package directions), drain, and transfer to the mixing bowl. Pour two-thirds of the pomodoro sauce over the pasta and stir with a large spoon. Add the Parmigiano and stir.

Plate in four bowls and finish each with a scoop of the remaining sauce, more Parmigiano, an additional good-looking basil leaf, and a drizzle of oil. Enjoy!

Lasagna Casalinga: Lasagna alla Boscaiola / **Lasagna from the Forest**

3 tablespoons extra-virgin olive oil

1 small shallot, finely chopped

2 cloves garlic

2 mild Italian pork sausages, casing removed and crumbled

¼ cup dry white wine

1½ pounds mixed seasonal mushrooms, trimmed and cut into 1-inch pieces

½ pound frozen petite peas

⅓ cup vegetable broth

Kosher salt and freshly ground black pepper

¼ cup unsalted butter, divided

Besciamella (recipe follows)

1 pound fresh lasagna sheets

¾ cup grated Parmigiano-Reggiano

Lasagna is unquestionably one of the most recognized Italian *primo piatto*. It comes in many forms and variations, although *lasagna alla Bolognese* is the most known version around the world, and for a good reason. It's always delicious.

Every time you make lasagna, you perform a *gesto di amore* (to quote my friend Viola Buitoni). When we opened Pasta Casalinga, we wanted to serve a lasagna available every day, but something different from lasagna alla Bolognese. Then I thought about *lasagna alla boscaiola*—lasagna from the forest—called this because of the mushrooms. A common Italian tomato-less lasagna, it's both delicate and succulent.

All the ingredients need to be cooled down, and ideally made the day before. The preparation is long but utterly worth it: an act of love indeed.

MAKES 6 SERVINGS

In a medium-large sauté pan over medium-low heat, warm the olive oil for a minute. Add the shallot and garlic, and sauté for 2 minutes, stirring to avoid burning. Add the sausage, making sure it is well crumbled. Increase the heat to medium and cook for 2 minutes, stirring occasionally. Add the wine and continue cooking for another 2 minutes.

Add the mushrooms, stirring for a minute. Stir in the peas, then pour in the vegetable broth. Season with salt and pepper to taste.

ANYTIME

Fresh lasagna sheets can be substituted with store-bought; just follow the cooking instructions on the package.

See page 34 for mushroom-cleaning instructions.

Cover, reduce the heat to medium-low, and cook for 10 to 15 minutes, or until the sauce is loose and not too thick.

Uncover, remove the garlic, and set aside.

Preheat the oven to 350 degrees F. Coat the bottom and sides of a 12-inch rectangular lasagna baking dish with the butter.

To build the lasagna, start with a thin layer of besciamella, spread evenly over the entire baking dish. Add a layer of the fresh lasagna sheets, making sure there are no gaps between the sheets. Cover with the sausage-mushroom sauce, another layer of besciamella, and a sprinkle of the Parmigiano. Repeat this layering four times. Finish with a top layer of besciamella, Parmigiano, and a few knobs of the remaining butter.

Bake for 40 minutes, or until crispy on top. Let it cool down for 10 minutes before cutting into squares and serving.

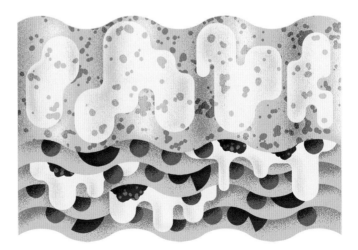

4 cups whole milk

½ cup unsalted butter

4 ounces all-purpose flour

¼ teaspoon freshly ground nutmeg

Kosher salt and ground white pepper

BESCIAMELLA

Originally invented by our cousins behind the Alps, who call it béchamel, *besciamella* is an essential component of several Italian *primi piatti*, as well as cannelloni and *pasta al forno* in all its variations. I love mine with a good amount of nutmeg and delicate white pepper.

MAKES ABOUT 4 CUPS

In a medium pot over medium heat, warm the milk, turning off the heat just before it starts to boil.

Meanwhile, in a medium saucepan over low heat, melt the butter. Once the butter is completely melted, turn off the heat, add the flour, and whisk constantly to create a roux.

Pour a scoop of the hot milk into the saucepan and continue to whisk energetically to obtain a smooth consistency. Turn the heat back on to medium-low and slowly add the rest of the milk. Cook, stirring constantly, for 5 to 7 minutes, or until the besciamella coats the back of a spoon.

Stir in the nutmeg, season with salt and pepper to taste, and let cool completely before layering the lasagna.

Acknowledgments

This book would have never been possible without the amazing women who fed me as a child back home in Italy—my mother, Gina, and my two grandmothers, Rosa and Michela. Their approach and movements in the kitchen were always natural and joyful, and they never actually taught me a single recipe. "Just watch and learn" was their motto. Simplicity and seasonality were at the heart of all their dishes, and this philosophy completely shaped my palate and upbringing. From them I derived my respect for ingredients and the belief that cooking itself is an expression of love and care for family and friends. In Italy the best way to show gratitude and respect is to invite someone to your house for a meal: homemade antipasti, *primi*, *secondi piatti*, *contorni*, and *dolci* are prepared, served, and consumed in this order and with enormous pride. I gladly inherited that.

A *grazie mille* goes to Piero Tantini and Marco Panichi of Godot, in Via Cartolerie, 12 Bologna, a restaurant where I worked during college two decades ago. I walked in green and learned what hospitality means. I felt proud and excited during all my work shifts, feeling as if I was part of something exceptional with incredible leaders and a winning team (Riccardo, Gloria, Beppe, Elena, Barbara, Andrea).

A thank-you to my precious mentor and dear friend Maria Coassin from Gelatiamo, who single-handedly created in Seattle not just a brand but a wonderful avenue for sharing real Italian pastries and gelato.

To Renee Erickson, a true inspiration in our community for cuisine and hospitality. Her commitment to sourcing ingredients and what she has built always make me feel that Seattle is truly an international city.

To Tom Douglas, who was outspoken and frank when I asked him for his thoughts about the Pasta Casalinga project, and who made me face all the possible challenges.

To Pietro Borghesi of Osteria la Spiga, for his fraternal love and endless conversations during good and difficult times.

To David Butler of Le Caviste, a sanctuary for after-hours rest over wine and conversation.

To Salvio Varchetta of Barolo for his constant support and friendship.

To Viola Buitoni, who taught me to *metterci la faccia*, to put yourself out there.

To my team, from the line cooks to the dishwashers to the front of the house: these recipes wouldn't be possible without all of you. And to Nathan Gottlieb, for his precious help when we opened Pasta Casalinga.

To my girls, Viola Rosa and Eva Luna, always the first tasters of a new menu. You are my daily motivation to be a work in progress.

ACKNOWLEDGMENTS

151

Resources

Here some of my favorite purveyors in Washington State. Sourcing and buying local means investing in our community by supporting our farmers, artisanal producers, and friends.

Cheese/Dairy
Beecher's Handmade Cheese, BeechersHandmadeCheese.com
Ferndale Farmstead, FerndaleFarmstead.com
Twin Sisters Creamery, TwinSistersCreamery.com

Grain/Flour
Bluebird Grain Farms, BluebirdGrainFarms.com
Cairnspring Mills, Cairnspring.com
Shepherd's Grain, ShepherdsGrain.com

Meat
Chehalis Valley Farms, www.chehalisvalleyfarm.com
Riccio's Sausage Company
Stonecrest Farm & Graziers, StonecrestonLopez.com

Produce/Forage
Alvarez Organic Farms, AlvarezOrganic.com
Billy's Gardens, BillysGardens.com
Foraged & Found Edibles, ForagedandFoundEdibles.com
Local Roots Farm, LocalRootsFarm.com
Red Dog Farm, RedDogFarm.net
Succession Wines, SuccessionWines.com
Wild Foragers, WildForagers.com

Seafood/Shellfish
Coleman Fish, ColemanFish.com
Hama Hama Oyster Company, HamaHamaOysters.com
Penn Cove Shellfish, PennCoveShellfish.com
Pike Place Fish Market, PikePlaceFish.com
Taylor Shellfish Farms, TaylorShellfishFarms.com

Index

Note: Page numbers in *italic* refer to photographs.

About the Author

Michela Tartaglia is a native Italian, born in the province of Turin, Piedmont. She moved to Seattle for a sabbatical year in 2006 after completing her master's degree in philosophy at Alma Mater Studiorum–University of Bologna, and has since made Seattle her adopted city. Her passion for linguistics and languages is captured in her first book, *Una Mela al Giorno*, published in Italy by Nomos Edizioni. She is a chef by heart, more than by trade. She cofounded Pasta Casalinga, an intimate lunch spot in the heart of Pike Place Market. Since its opening in 2018, Pasta Casalinga has become a lunch destination for locals and visitors alike. She lives in North Beach with her two daughters, Viola Rosa and Eva Luna.

ABOUT THE PHOTOGRAPHER

Kyle Johnson is a photographer hailing from the Pacific Northwest. His aesthetic pairs textured natural settings with a distinct photographic perspective. Some of his recent clients include the *New York Times*, *Bon Appétit*, *Condé Nast Traveler*, and *WSJ. Magazine*.

ABOUT THE ILLUSTRATOR

Daniele Simonelli is a full-time freelance illustrator based in the eternal City of Rome, from where he has fought against the use of clipart for ten years (and counting) and has created work for editorial, advertising, and design industries with international clients.

Printed in China

SASQUATCH BOOKS with colophon is a registered trademark of Penguin Random House LLC

27 26 25 24 23   9 8 7 6 5 4 3 2 1

Editor: Jen Worick / Production editor: Rachelle Longé McGhee
Designer: Anna Goldstein / Photographer: Kyle Johnson
Illustrator: Daniele Simonelli

Library of Congress Cataloging-in-Publication Data
Names: Tartaglia, Michela, author. | Johnson, Kyle (Photographer)
   photographer. | Simonelli, Daniele, illustrator.
Title: Pasta for all seasons : dishes that celebrate the flavors of Italy
   and the bounty of the Pacific Northwest / Michela Tartaglia ;
   photography by Kyle Johnson ; illustrations by Daniele Simonelli.
Description: Seattle, WA : Sasquatch Books, [2023] | Includes index. |
Identifiers: LCCN 2022038683 (print) | LCCN 2022038684 (ebook) | ISBN
   9781632174277 (hardcover) | ISBN 9781632174284 (epub)
Subjects: LCSH: Cooking, Italian. | Cooking (Pasta) | Seasonal cooking. |
   LCGFT: Cookbooks.
Classification: LCC TX723 .T35 2023 (print) | LCC TX723 (ebook) | DDC
   641.5945--dc23/eng/20220821
LC record available at https://lccn.loc.gov/2022038683
LC ebook record available at https://lccn.loc.gov/2022038684

The recipes contained in this book have been created for the ingredients and techniques indicated. Neither publisher nor author is responsible for your specific health or allergy needs that may require supervision. Nor are publisher and author responsible for any adverse reactions you may have to the recipes contained in the book, whether you follow them as written or modify them to suit your personal dietary needs or tastes.

ISBN: 978-1-63217-427-7

Sasquatch Books / 1325 Fourth Avenue, Suite 1025 / Seattle, WA 98101

SasquatchBooks.com

MIX
Paper | Supporting responsible forestry
FSC® C008047